COLOMBIA 2016 HUMAN RIGHTS REPORT

EXECUTIVE SUMMARY

Colombia is a constitutional, multiparty republic. In June 2014 voters re-elected Juan Manuel Santos president in elections that observers considered free and fair. On August 24, the government and the Revolutionary Armed Forces of Colombia (FARC), the country's largest guerrilla insurgency group, reached agreement on a final peace accord covering rural reform; political participation; illicit drugs; victims (including transitional justice); end of conflict; and implementation, verification, and public approval. The parties signed the accord September 26. In an October 2 plebiscite, however, the public narrowly rejected the agreement, resulting in the initiation of an inclusive national dialogue aimed at reaching a revised accord. The government and the FARC announced November 12 a revised peace accord, which drew from a national dialogue convoked by President Juan Manuel Santos following the October 2 vote. The Colombian congress approved the revised peace accord November 30.

Civilian authorities generally maintained effective control over security forces.

The three most prevalent human rights problems in the country were impunity, forced displacement, and societal discrimination. An inefficient justice system, with a judiciary in which officials were subjected to threats and intimidation, limited the government's ability to prosecute effectively many individuals accused of human rights abuses, including high-level state agents and former members of paramilitary groups. The presence of drug traffickers, guerrilla fighters, and other illegal armed groups continued to displace predominantly poor and rural populations. Violence and societal discrimination against women; lesbian, gay, bisexual, transgender, and intersex (LGBTI) persons; indigenous persons; and Afro-Colombians often restricted the ability of these groups to exercise their rights.

Other significant human rights problems continued, including extrajudicial and unlawful killings; unauthorized military collaboration with members of illegal armed groups; forced disappearances; overcrowded and insecure prisons; harassment and attacks against human rights groups and activists, including death threats and killings; violence against women and girls; trafficking in persons; and illegal child labor.

The government continued efforts to prosecute and punish perpetrators of abuses, including members of the security services. It increased resources for the Attorney

General's Office, devoted significant resources to human rights cases, and employed a contextual analysis strategy to analyze human rights and other cases systematically. Nonetheless, the system struggled to close out cases quickly and efficiently.

Despite peace negotiations with the FARC, illegal armed groups--including the National Liberation Army (ELN), as well as organized crime groups (some of which contained former paramilitary members)--continued to commit numerous human rights abuses, including the following: political killings; killings of members of the public security forces and local officials; widespread use of land mines and improvised explosive devices (IEDs); kidnappings and forced disappearances; sexual and gender-based violence; subornation and intimidation of judges, prosecutors, and witnesses; infringement on citizens' privacy rights; restrictions on freedom of movement; widespread recruitment and use of child soldiers; and killings, harassment, and intimidation of human rights activists, teachers, and trade unionists. Illegal armed groups continued to be responsible for most instances of forced displacement in the country.

Section 1. Respect for the Integrity of the Person, Including Freedom from:

a. Arbitrary Deprivation of Life and other Unlawful or Politically Motivated Killings

There were reports the government or its agents committed arbitrary or unlawful killings, and related investigations and prosecutions proceeded slowly (see section 1.g.).

There was a reduction in violence due to progress in the peace process between the government and the FARC, including the implementation of a bilateral ceasefire August 29. The UN Office of the High Commissioner for Human Rights (OHCHR) 2015 annual report stated the peace negotiations "prevented many human rights violations." During the year the Conflict Analysis Research Center (CERAC) reported levels of violence in the country fell to their lowest in 52 years in terms of the number of victims, combatants killed and injured, and the number of violent acts. According to CERAC, offensive actions against the FARC fell 98 percent, combat between the armed forces and the FARC dropped by 91 percent, overall civilian casualties fell by 98 percent, and overall combatant deaths dropped by 94 percent. The OHCHR and CERAC attributed these trends to confidence-building measures, such as the unilateral ceasefire by the FARC, and the high level of compliance with the bilateral ceasefire.

In February members of the army allegedly killed Gilberto de Jesus Quintero in the department of Antioquia. Security forces claimed that Quintero was a suspected member of the ELN, according to media. As of October 20, the government had failed to investigate the case.

From January 1 through July, the Attorney General's Office registered 291 new cases of alleged aggravated homicides by state agents. During the same period, authorities formally accused 393 members of the security forces and arrested 445 for aggravated homicide or homicide of a civilian, 45 of them for crimes that occurred prior to 2015.

There were developments in efforts to hold officials accountable in false positive cases, in which thousands of civilians were allegedly killed and falsely presented as guerrilla combatants in the late 1990s to mid-2000s. In February Colonel Robinson Gonzalez del Rio, convicted and sentenced in 2015 to a total of 67 years in prison and a fine of more than 1.8 billion Colombian Pesos (COP) ($6 million) for the unlawful killing of 34 civilians presented as "false positives," was sentenced to an additional 37 years and six months in prison for the deaths of Javier Moreno and Janio Sepulveda in 2007 in Caldas Department.

Investigations of generals allegedly implicated in false positive cases continued. In April 2015 the former attorney general stated publicly that his office was investigating 22 generals for alleged involvement in false positives cases. In August the Attorney General's Office subsequently clarified that the number of investigations against generals (including retired generals) involving homicides was actually 15, rather than 22. As of August the Attorney General's Office stated 12 cases involving generals were in the preliminary investigation phase, and investigations against three generals had been closed.

On March 28, the Attorney General's Office announced General Henry William Torres Escalante and former army commander general Mario Montoya Uribe would be formally charged for their alleged connections to false positive cases. The attorney general found that General Torres Escalante was pivotal in the homicide of Daniel Torres Arciniegas and his son Roque Julio Torres, who were falsely presented as FARC members killed in combat in 2007. On March 28, authorities arrested Torres Escalante, which marked the first instance an active-duty general faced criminal charges related to the false positives scandal. He was called to trial in August.

General Montoya faced charges in connection with his alleged involvement in seven false positive cases and awaited arraignment as of mid-October. He was accused of supporting paramilitary groups and actions in operations such as Operation Orion, a 2002 military offensive against guerrillas in Medellin.

On June 1, Commander of the Armed Forces General Mejia and Minister of Defense Villegas publicly honored Sergeant Carlos Mora, a whistleblower in the false positives scandal. Mejia urged the army's leadership to hold themselves and their units to the highest standards of transparency and to respect human rights and international humanitarian law.

The OHCHR reported it registered seven possible cases of "illegal deprivation of the right to life" alleged to have been committed by security force members from January 1 through July 31. In several cases military officials stated they believed an individual was fighting on behalf of the FARC, while community members claimed the victim was not a combatant. In other cases military officials stated the killings were military mistakes.

Human rights organizations, victims, and government investigators accused some members of government security forces, including enlisted personnel, noncommissioned officers, and officers, of collaborating with or tolerating the activities of organized criminal gangs, which included some former paramilitary members.

According to the Attorney General's Office, during the year through September 30, authorities arrested and charged 24 government employees, including 23 members of the National Police, with having links to illegal armed groups, mainly the group known as Gulf Clan, previously known as Clan Usuga or the Gaitanista Self-Defense Forces of Colombia.

On January 17, in Caceres, Antioquia Department, Melisa Espitia Mazo, a pregnant 14-year-old, was killed during a military operation against criminal groups. The army recognized its responsibility in Espitia's death and apologized for what it stated was a military error. The Antioquia branch of the Attorney General's Office launched an investigation to clarify the circumstances of the death; as of October, there were no arrests or charges related to the case.

Investigations of past killings proceeded, albeit slowly. The Attorney General's Office reported that during the year through July, it obtained 117 new convictions of security force members in cases involving homicide of a "protected person" (i.e., civilians and others accorded such status under international humanitarian law), 161 new convictions in cases involving aggravated homicide, and 191 new convictions in cases involving "simple homicide" committed by security force members.

On March 16, two former paramilitary members, Dalson Lopez Simanca and Jose Luis Conrado Perez, were sentenced to 40 years' imprisonment for their involvement in the 1995 El Aracatazzo massacre, in the municipality of Chigorodo, in which members of the military, along with members of paramilitary groups, allegedly tortured and killed 18 civilians.

On March 1, the Justice and Peace Tribunal, following an investigation begun in 2014, forwarded evidence to the Attorney General's Office to initiate investigations against retired generals Oscar Botero Cardona and German Morantes Hernandez for human rights violations.

The Colombia-Europe-United States Coordination Group and other nongovernmental organizations (NGOs) considered organized criminal bands to be a continuation of former paramilitary groups and in some cases accused elements of the government of collaborating with those groups to commit human rights violations. The government acknowledged that some former paramilitary members were active in organized criminal gangs but noted the gangs lacked the national, unified command structure and explicit ideological agenda that defined past paramilitary groups, including the disbanded United Self-Defense Forces of Colombia (AUC). The NGOs also included killings by these groups in their definition of "unlawful killings" (see section 1.g.).

According to the NGO Landmine Monitor, nonstate actors, particularly the ELN, planted IEDs and land mines (see section 1.g.).

Guerrillas, notably the ELN, committed unlawful killings. Organized criminal groups (some of which included former members of paramilitary groups) committed numerous political and unlawful killings, primarily in areas under dispute with guerrillas or without a strong government presence (see section 1.g.).

The investigation into the killing in 2012 of land restitution leader Manuel Ruiz and his son, Samir, continued under the direction of the Office of the Attorney General's National Directorate for Human Rights and International Humanitarian Law. On May 4, Manuel's and Samir's bodies were exhumed in coordination with the Justice and Peace Commission, international observers, and local leaders.

b. Disappearance

Forced disappearances, many of them politically motivated, continued to occur. Although the exact number of people disappeared remained unknown, there were at least 100,000 cases of disappearances during the half-century of conflict, according to the National Search Commission. From January 1 through the end of July, 48 victims of forced disappearances were found alive and 20 were found dead. The government did not provide information on the number of disappearances and forced disappearances registered.

The Attorney General's Office did not provide information on the number of new convictions in forced disappearance cases involving members of the security forces.

There were developments in efforts to provide reparations to families of disappeared victims of the 1985 military occupation of the Justice Palace in Bogota. In October the Attorney General's Office returned the remains of William Arturo Almonacid and Cristina del Pilar Guarin, two of the disappeared victims, to their families. The State Council ordered the Ministry of Defense to pay compensation to the family of disappeared victim Gloria Anzola de Lanao, in the amount of nearly COP 1.6 billion ($5,500,000). Lanao's body remained missing.

As part of a peace process confidence-building measure, the FARC agreed in October 2015 to search for those missing in the conflict. The government agreed to accelerate the identification of anonymous victims killed in security operations and extrajudicial killings, and to turn over their remains to family members. The parties also agreed to create a new search unit for the missing, with support from the International Committee of the Red Cross (ICRC).

The ELN, organized criminal gangs, and common criminals continued to kidnap persons, both for ransom and for political reasons (see section 1.g.). On February 4, the ELN kidnapped Jair de Jesus Villar, a military official, at a power plant in Antioquia Department. Villar was released in March, along with civilian Ramon Jose Cabrales, who was kidnapped in September 2015. In April former representative Odin Sanchez offered himself as a hostage to the ELN in exchange for the release of his brother, former Choco governor Patrocino Sanchez, who had been in ELN custody since 2014; however, as of November 7, Sanchez remained in custody. Between May 21 and May 24, the ELN abducted three journalists in Catatumbo. They were released May 27.

The Unified Action Groups for Personal Liberty--military and police entities formed to combat kidnapping and extortion--and other security force elements freed 33 hostages in the first seven months of the year. The government reported that two kidnapping victims died in captivity during the year through July. During that period nine kidnapping victims escaped from their captors, and 70 were released by their captors.

c. Torture and Other Cruel, Inhuman, or Degrading Treatment or Punishment

Although the law prohibits such practices, there were reports that police, military personnel, and prison guards sometimes committed abuses. Members of the military and police accused of torture generally were tried in civilian rather than military courts. The NGO Center for Research and Education of the Populace (CINEP) reported that during the year through September 9, security forces were allegedly involved in 13 cases of torture.

From January through July, the Attorney General's Office charged 25 members of the security forces (23 police and two military members) with torture; 14 of the cases occurred prior to 2016. The Attorney General's Office reported 12 convictions of members of the armed forces and no convictions of members of illegal armed groups in cases of torture during the year through June.

CINEP reported criminal bands were responsible for eight documented cases of torture through September 9. In nine other documented cases, CINEP was not able to identify the party responsible for the abuses.

According to NGOs working with the prison community, there were numerous allegations of sexual and physical violence committed by guards and other inmates.

Prison and Detention Center Conditions

With the exception of new facilities, prisons and detention centers were overcrowded, lacked adequate sanitation, and provided poor health care and other basic facilities. Poor training of officials remained a problem throughout the prison system.

<u>Physical Conditions</u>: The national prisons had a design capacity of 78,055 prisoners but held 121,157 inmates (112,927 men and 8,230 women). Overcrowding existed in men's as well as women's prisons. The National Prison Institute (INPEC) operated the national prisons and oversaw the jails.

On August 23, the Constitutional Court ordered the Bogota Metropolitan Police to cease using buses, parks, and other public spaces as temporary detention centers. The court also ordered INPEC to treat inmates and detainees in a dignified manner.

The law prohibits holding pretrial detainees with convicted prisoners, although this sometimes occurred.

The Superior Judiciary Council stated that the maximum time that a person may remain in judicial detention facilities is three days. The same rules apply to jails located inside police stations. These regulations were often not carried out.

The practice of preventive detention, in combination with inefficiencies in the judicial system, continued to exacerbate overcrowding. In April the Constitutional Court ruled all suspects jailed longer than the legally allowed period without being tried should be released on July 7. In June Congress approved a provisional bill extending the legal time a crime suspect could be held in jail, preventing the release from prison of approximately 20,000 crime suspects.

The Inspector General's Office continued to investigate allegations that some prison guards routinely used excessive force and treated inmates brutally. Through September it conducted 125 investigations, 71 of which concluded and 54 of which remained in the investigation phase.

Many prisoners continued to face difficulties receiving adequate medical care. Nutrition and water quality were deficient and contributed to the overall poor health of many inmates. Inmates claimed authorities routinely rationed water in many facilities. In May, INPEC and Justice Minister Jorge Londono declared an emergency in the country's prisons due to the deterioration of health-care conditions. The ministry explained that the state of emergency would enable the implementation of an action plan to address deficiencies in health care for prisoners, to include the creation of health brigades and the prompt execution of maintenance projects related to health-care provision.

INPEC's physical structures were in generally poor repair. The Inspector General's Office noted some facilities had poor ventilation and overtaxed sanitary systems. Prisoners in some high-altitude facilities complained of inadequate blankets and clothing, while prisoners in tropical facilities complained that overcrowding and insufficient ventilation contributed to high temperatures in prison cells. Some prisoners slept on floors without mattresses, while others shared cots in overcrowded cells.

Administration: INPEC used a centrally managed electronic database with regular updates, and each prison also had its own local database. Foreign diplomatic observers, however, found that the information in both systems often was not well coordinated, resulting in delays in locating foreign detainees, especially dual nationals who had both Colombian and foreign citizenships.

Prisoners generally could submit complaints to judicial authorities, request investigations of inhuman conditions, and request that third parties from local NGOs or government entities, such as the Ombudsman's Office, represent them in legal matters and aid them in seeking an investigation of prison conditions. Authorities investigated prisoner complaints of inhuman conditions, including complaints of prison guards soliciting bribes from inmates, but some prisoners asserted the investigations were slow and the results were not accessible to the public.

Independent Monitoring: The government permitted independent monitoring of prison conditions by local and international human rights groups that exercised a high degree of independence. INPEC required a three-day notice before granting consular access. Some NGOs complained that authorities, without adequate explanation, denied them access to visit prisoners.

Improvements: INPEC launched a new 2016 Anticorruption and Citizen Services Plan with the goal of creating a culture of legality and transparency and promoting new institutional practices, such as the concept of shared responsibility and self-regulation among public servants, citizens, and prison stakeholder groups. INPEC continued a campaign to raise awareness and strengthen a culture of human rights within the institution. Through August 12, a total of 221 prison officials received human rights training. The government also continued a pilot program with local universities and other organizations to provide distance learning for inmates. More than 1,000 inmates participated in the program through July.

d. Arbitrary Arrest or Detention

Although the law prohibits arbitrary arrest and detention, there were allegations that authorities detained citizens arbitrarily. CINEP reported 176 cases of arbitrary detention committed by state security forces during the year through September 9 (six committed by the attorney general's Corps of Technical Investigators (CTI), 22 by the armed forces, and 148 by police).

Role of the Police and Security Apparatus

The Colombian National Police (CNP) is responsible for internal law enforcement and is under the jurisdiction of the Ministry of Defense. The Migration Directorate, part of the Ministry of Foreign Affairs, is the immigration authority. The CNP shares law enforcement investigatory duties with the CTI. In addition to its responsibility to defend the country against external threats, the army shares limited responsibility for law enforcement and maintenance of order within the country. For example, military units sometimes provided logistical support and security for criminal investigators to collect evidence in high-conflict or remote areas. The government continued to expand education and training of the armed forces in human rights and international humanitarian law.

By law the Attorney General's Office is the main entity responsible for investigating allegations of human rights abuses by security forces. Of these alleged abuses, extrajudicial killings were the highest profile and most controversial. The CTI, which consists of civilian authorities under the Attorney General's Office, typically investigated deaths resulting from action by security forces when there were allegations of foul play. In some cases the first responders were CNP members, who then investigated the death. Some NGOs complained that military investigators, not members of the Attorney General's Office, were sometimes the first responders in cases of deaths resulting from actions of security forces and might make decisions about possible foul play.

The government made improvements in investigating and trying abuses, but NGO claims continued of impunity for security force members. This was due in some cases to obstruction of justice, opacity in the process by which cases are investigated and prosecuted in the military justice system, and a lack of resources for investigations. Inadequate protection of witnesses and investigators, delay tactics by defense attorneys, the judiciary's failure to exert appropriate controls over dockets and case progress, and inadequate coordination among government entities that sometimes allowed statutes of limitations to expire, resulting in a defendant's release from jail before trial were also significant obstacles.

The military functions under both the old inquisitorial and a newer accusatory system. The military had not trained its criminal justice actors to operate under the accusatory system, which they were to begin to implement during the year. The military also had not developed an interinstitutional strategy for the recruiting, hiring, or training investigators, crime scene technicians, or forensic specialists, which is required under the accusatory system. As such, the military justice system did not exercise criminal investigative authority; all new criminal investigations duties are conducted by CNP judicial police investigators.

The Attorney General's Office continued investigations into numerous generals and field-grade officers for involvement in alleged false positive cases and other abuses (see section 1.a.).

Arrest Procedures and Treatment of Detainees

Authorities must bring detained persons before a judge within 36 hours to determine the validity of the detention, bring formal charges within 30 days, and start a trial within 90 days of the initial detention. Bail is generally available except for serious accusations, such as murder, rebellion, or narcotics trafficking. Public defenders contracted by the Office of the Ombudsman assisted indigent defendants. Detainees received prompt access to legal counsel and family members as provided for by law. Authorities generally respected these rights.

Arbitrary Arrest: The law prohibits arbitrary arrest and detention; however, this requirement was not always respected. NGOs characterized some arrests as arbitrary detention: arrests allegedly based on tips from informants about persons linked to guerrilla activities, detentions by members of the security forces without a judicial order, detentions based on administrative authority, detentions during military operations or at roadblocks, large-scale detentions, and detentions of persons while they were "exercising their fundamental rights."

Pretrial Detention: The judicial process moved slowly, and the civilian judicial system suffered from a significant backlog of cases, which led to large numbers of pretrial detainees. The failure of many local military commanders and jail supervisors to keep mandatory detention records or follow notification procedures made accounting for all detainees difficult. No information was available on the percent of detainees in pretrial detention or the average length of time detainees spent in pretrial detention. In some cases detainees were released without a trial because they already served more than one-third of the maximum sentence that corresponded to their charges.

Civil society groups complained that authorities subjected some community leaders to extended pretrial detention.

<u>Detainee's Ability to Challenge Lawfulness of Detention before a Court</u>: Article 30 of the constitution guarantees habeas corpus review for all detainees. Such reviews must be completed within 36 hours. In the case of an illegal deprivation of freedom or illegal detention, Article 90 of the constitution provides for the government to compensate the victim.

e. Denial of Fair Public Trial

The law provides for an independent judiciary, and the government generally respected judicial independence. Much of the judicial system was overburdened and inefficient, and subornation and intimidation of judges, prosecutors, and witnesses hindered judicial functioning. The Attorney General's Office had a witness protection program for criminal cases, but some of those who did not enter the program allegedly remained vulnerable to intimidation, and many refused to testify.

The military justice system may investigate and prosecute active-duty military and police personnel for crimes "related to acts of military service." According to the Ministry of Defense, human rights abuses are not considered acts related to military service. The military penal code specifically excludes civilians from military jurisdiction, and civilian courts must try retired military and police personnel, but military courts are responsible for service-related acts committed prior to retirement.

According to domestic NGOs, more than 10 initiatives for military justice reform were presented in the previous five years, but few were enacted, due to removal from the legislative process because of procedural problems or rejection by the Constitutional Court. In 2015 the government dropped proposed jurisdictional adjustments from its proposed military justice reform legislation to address concerns that the legislation could lead to some human rights cases being heard by military courts. Despite explicit declarations from officials to the contrary, some NGOs remained concerned that military justice reform efforts may allow certain human rights cases to fall within the military justice system's jurisdiction.

According to the Supreme Judicial Council, a body that settles jurisdictional questions between the military and civilian justice systems, from January 1 to July, authorities assigned to the civilian justice system 61 of 74 homicide cases reviewed for jurisdiction. During the same period, they assigned four cases to the military justice system. The magistrates abstained from ruling on the proper jurisdiction in the remaining nine cases, in which they determined that they either did not have enough information to rule or that a conflict of interest with the case prevented them from ruling.

The military penal code denies commanders the power to impose military justice discipline on, and extends legal protection to, service members who refuse to obey orders to commit human rights abuses. The army also has discretionary authority to dismiss personnel implicated in human rights abuses.

The Inspector General's Office investigates allegations of misconduct by public employees, including members of government security forces. In addition to conducting its own investigations, the Inspector General's Office referred all cases of human rights violations it received to the attorney general's Human Rights Unit for separate criminal proceedings. As of July 31, the Inspector General's Office opened 21 disciplinary processes against members of the armed forces and police for human rights offenses, resulting in 12 preliminary investigations and nine disciplinary investigations, to which 59 members of the army and one member of the National Police were linked. Additionally, the Office of Delegated Disciplinary Inspector General for the Armed Forces reported that through August, it initiated 13 disciplinary investigations for alleged offenses. Thirty-four individuals were linked to these cases.

Trial Procedures

While the government began implementing an accusatory system of justice in 2008, the use of delay tactics by defense lawyers to slow or impede proceedings, prosecutors' heavy caseloads, and other factors diminished the anticipated increased efficiencies and other benefits of adopting the adversarial model. Under the existing criminal procedure code, the prosecutor presents an accusation and evidence before an impartial judge at an oral, public trial. The defendant is presumed innocent until proven guilty beyond a reasonable doubt and has the right to confront the trial evidence and witnesses against him, present his own evidence, and communicate with an attorney of choice (or have one provided at public expense). Defendants have adequate time and facilities to prepare their defense and may access government-held evidence during the trial stage. Defendants are not compelled to testify or confess guilt and have the right to appeal their proceedings. Although defendants have the right to an interpreter, the court system lacked interpreters for less-commonly encountered languages. Crimes committed before 2008 are processed under the prior written inquisitorial system in which the prosecutor is an investigating magistrate who investigates, determines evidence, and makes a finding of guilt or innocence. In those cases the trial consists of the presentation of evidence and finding of guilt or innocence to a judge for ratification or rejection.

In the military justice system, military judges preside over courts-martial. Counsel may represent the accused and call witnesses, but most fact-finding takes place during the investigative stage. Military trial judges issue rulings within eight days of a court-martial hearing. Representatives of the civilian Inspector General's Office are required to be present at courts-martial.

Criminal procedure within the military justice system includes elements of the inquisitorial and accusatory systems. Defendants are considered innocent until proven guilty and have the right to timely consultation with counsel. The law provides for the right to a fair trial, and an independent judiciary generally enforced this right.

Political Prisoners and Detainees

The government declared that it did not hold political prisoners. Authorities did hold some members of human rights advocacy groups on charges of conspiracy, rebellion, or terrorism, which the groups described as government harassment tactics against human rights advocates. The government did not provide information on the number of detainees in prisons, jails, or under house arrest who were accused or convicted of rebellion or aiding and abetting the insurgency. The government provided the ICRC regular access to these prisoners.

Civil Judicial Procedures and Remedies

Citizens may sue a government agent or entity in the Administrative Court of Litigation for damages resulting from a human rights violation. Although critics complained of delays in the process, the court generally was considered impartial and effective. Cases involving violations of an individual's human rights may be submitted through petitions by individuals or organizations to the Inter-American Commission of Human Rights, which in turn may submit the case to the Inter-American Court on Human Rights. The court may order civil remedies, including fair compensation to the individual injured.

Property Restitution

The 2011 Victims' and Land Restitution Law (Victims' Law) continues to provide a legal basis for assistance and reparations to persons, including victims of the government, but the government admitted that the pace of restitution was slow. The Administrative Department for Social Prosperity (DPS) handles problems related to victims, poverty, consolidation, historical memory, and protection of children and adolescents. The Victims' Unit of the DPS has the governmental lead on attention to victims. From 2011 through August 1, 2016, a total of 7,844,527 victims registered with the Victims' Unit. Of these, 6,883,513 were victims of forced displacement, with 17,976 registered during the year through August 1. The government did not provide information on the number of those registered who received some form of assistance. There were 340 registered cases of collective reparations. Both individual and collective reparations are mandated by the Victims' Law, however, the original budget for implementation of the law contemplated only 4.5 million victims. The Land Restitution Unit, a semiautonomous entity in the Ministry of Agriculture, is responsible for returning land to displaced victims of conflict. As of August 19, the government received 93,686 land restitution claims, of which more than 50,903 claims fell within the government's target areas for restitution and went into active review. The government reported as of the same date, courts handed down 1,948 decisions on land restitution, corresponding to affirmative decisions in 3,980 cases with 23,085 beneficiaries. The Inspector General's Office intervened to support land claimants in 679 cases through July, providing support in the administrative, judicial, and post-ruling phases in order to ensure the effective implementation of victims' right to integral reparation.

Through July the Land Restitution Unit approved three requests for collective restitution of ethnic territories or individual restitution claims, corresponding to 130,972 acres benefitting 2,473 families and 12,365 persons. Of the 93,686 individual cases received through July, 2,888 belonged to individuals self-identified as Afro-Colombian, 1,624 to individuals self-identified as indigenous, and 638 to individuals self-identified as pertaining to other ethnic groups.

f. Arbitrary or Unlawful Interference with Privacy, Family, Home, or Correspondence

The law prohibits such actions, but there were allegations that the government failed to respect these prohibitions. Government authorities generally need a judicial order to intercept mail or e-mail, or monitor telephone conversations, including in prisons. Government intelligence agencies investigating terrorist organizations sometimes monitored telephone conversations without judicial authorization, but evidence obtained in such a manner may not be used in court.

During the year through July, the Attorney General's Office initiated three new criminal investigations of government agents for illegal monitoring activities. During the year through September, the Inspector General's Office reported it had not initiated any disciplinary investigations of public servants accused of illegal monitoring activities.

In February the Inspector General's Office opened an investigation into journalist Vicky Davila's accusations that police had been monitoring her communications, including trailing and wiretapping her and her reporting team, since 2014.

An investigation continued into abuses by the Army Intelligence Unit, known by its code name "Andromeda." *Semana* magazine alleged that the unit illegally wiretapped personal telephones of peace negotiators belonging to both the government and FARC negotiating teams. General Mauricio Forero, former head of the military's intelligence center, left the army on April 1 for alleged connections to Andromeda. As of October he had not been charged or arrested in connection with these allegations.

On March 10, the Attorney General's Office pressed charges against David Parra Amin, a police sergeant assigned to the Section of Criminal Investigations in Bogota, for his alleged role as the liaison between Andres Sepulveda, convicted in 2015 for tapping into communications of peace negotiating teams and government officials, and the Bogota Metropolitan Police.

On August 29, attorneys for Martha Ines Leal, former director of operations of the dismantled Administrative Department of Security (DAS); Jorge Lagos, former DAS intelligence director; and Fernando Tabares, former DAS counterintelligence director, submitted to the Inter-American Commission on Human Rights allegations that the Attorney General's Office placed undue pressure on them in order to coerce them into testifying in the DAS illegal surveillance case. The DAS allegedly engaged in illegal surveillance of high court magistrates, journalists, human rights organizations and activists, opposition leaders, and the vice presidency.

In its annual report published in March, the OHCHR registered 80 complaints of illegal surveillance of human rights defenders and social activists in 2015. While statistics for 2016 were unavailable as of October, NGOs continued to accuse domestic intelligence or security entities of spying on lawyers and human rights defenders, threatening them, and breaking into their homes or offices to steal information.

The government continued to use voluntary civilian informants to identify terrorists, report terrorist activities, and gather information on criminal gangs. Some national and international human rights groups criticized this practice as subject to abuse and a threat to privacy and other civil liberties. The government maintained that the practice was in accordance with the "principle of solidarity" outlined in the constitution and that the Comptroller General's Office strictly regulated payments to such informants.

g. Abuses in Internal Conflict

Following the rejection of the initial accord between the government and the FARC in an October 2 plebiscite, the government, leaders of the plebiscite "No" campaign, and the FARC engaged in a national dialogue that led to a revised accord announced November 12. The government and the FARC signed the revised peace accord November 24, and the congress ratified the agreement November 30. President Santos and the FARC leadership announced December 1 was "D-Day," triggering a 180-day deadline for the FARC to begin demobilization and disarmament in UN-monitored concentration zones throughout Colombia. A UN mission was monitoring, as of December 15, the bilateral ceasefire and cessation of hostilities the parties established August 29. The country's internal armed conflict with the ELN, organized criminal groups, and narcotics traffickers continued. On May 30, the government announced an agenda for formal peace negotiations with the ELN. They had not yet begun as of the end of the year.

During the year reports of human rights abuses occurred in the context of the conflict and narcotics trafficking.

Guerrilla group members continued to demobilize on an individual basis. In the first eight months of the year, according to the Ministry of Defense, 559 members of guerrilla groups demobilized, reflecting a 32 percent reduction in FARC demobilizations but a 52 percent increase in ELN demobilizations over the same period in 2015 (375 from the FARC, 179 from the ELN, and five from other dissident groups). The Organization of American States verified all stages of demobilization and reintegration into society of former combatants from the guerrilla and former paramilitary groups.

Through August 22, the Human Rights Directorate of the Ministry of Defense, in conjunction with the ICRC, conducted 16 human rights training sessions for 980 ministry personnel. In September the International Defense Institute for Legal Studies conducted training for 25 military and police officials, as well as nonmilitary personnel, with the objective of strengthening the working relationships between unit leaders and their operational legal advisers.

Implementation of the 2005 Justice and Peace Law (JPL) continued. The Justice and Peace Unit in the Attorney General's Office is responsible for the required investigation and prosecution of demobilized persons, and an interagency commission on justice and peace coordinates implementation. Participants in the justice and peace process may receive reduced sentences of five to eight years in prison if they comply with the terms of the JPL. Information provided in voluntary confessions as part of the JPL also initiated investigations of politicians, military members, major agricultural producers, and government officials' past ties to paramilitary forces. Some of the investigations resulted in prosecutions and convictions.

As of June 2015, the government reported a total of 5,024 former paramilitary and guerrilla defendants participated in confession hearings. During these sessions the defendants confessed to 57,207 crimes, and information was obtained that resulted in the exhumation of 978 victims. As of the same date, 813 defendants were formally charged in presentations before the courts by the Office of the Attorney General's Justice and Peace Unit. During 2015 through June, 1,106 defendants reached their eight-year maximum incarceration dates under the agreed arrangement, and authorities released 39 for reintegration into society. The Justice and Peace Unit moved to expel from the JPL process those defendants who do not fully comply by confessing crimes, turning over illegally acquired assets, and ceasing their criminal activity. Updated information for 2016 was not available by November.

Application of the JPL continued to face many challenges. Thousands of former paramilitary members remained in legal limbo due to resource and capacity constraints at the Attorney General's Office. There was also little land or money confiscated from former paramilitary leaders to be used for required victim reparations.

The creation of a truth-seeking mechanism in Law 1424 of 2010 (the Legal Status for Former Combatants Law) requires demobilized paramilitary fighters who did not commit crimes against humanity to provide testimony on the actions and structures of illegal armed groups to the Center for Historical Memory as a requirement for being granted legal status and suspended sentences for lesser crimes. The law also provides for establishing and institutionalizing formal archives, creating a Center for Historical Memory for collecting oral testimony and material documentation concerning violations of international human rights norms and law, and constructing the National Museum of Memory in consultation with victims. In a report published in 2013, the Center for Historical Memory documented the killing of at least 220,000 citizens in the context of the armed conflict from 1958 to 2012, 80 percent of whom were unarmed civilians.

Civil society groups also accused all sides of the armed conflict of having engaged in activities that targeted noncombatant civilians, including women and children.

Killings: Security forces were implicated in alleged unlawful killings. CINEP reported there were 19 such killings during the year through September 9 (eight committed by police, five by the army, one by the navy, and five by INPEC).

Guerrilla groups and criminal organizations were also implicated in unlawful killings during the year, but precise numbers were not provided by the government. On August 26, media reported that ELN members in Barbacoas, Narino, killed Camilo Roberto Taicus Bisbucus, an indigenous member of the Awa community.

According to the human rights advocacy NGO Minga, no progress had been made in the 2008 Soacha extrajudicial killings scandal, and all five cases remained in the initial investigation stage at the Attorney General's Office. The cases of three more victims were in the evidentiary stage, that of another victim was pending plea bargain agreements with four soldiers who accepted their responsibility in the crimes, and the cases of five additional victims were in final allegation hearings. As of August 29, there were no convictions.

Abductions: Criminal and illegal armed elements engaged in abductions. According to the NGO Fundacion Pais Libre, between January 1, 2015 and June 30, 2016, criminals and illegal armed groups kidnapped 320 persons, including 179 for extortion. Pais Libre also reported that authorities rescued 91 kidnapping victims; captors released 179, 20 were presumed to remain in captivity, three were released due to pressure by authorities, 22 escaped, and five died in captivity. ELN guerrillas continued to take hostages for ransom and for political reasons. The government reported that the ELN kidnapped 12 persons during the first seven months of the year. As of November 7, at least one civilian remained in ELN captivity.

The ICRC reported that from January 1 through November 16, it participated in 10 operations to release persons in the hands of nonstate actors, eight held by the ELN, and two held by the FARC.

Through July 21, the Attorney General's Office reported one conviction for abductions committed by members of the FARC and no convictions for abductions committed by members of the ELN.

Physical Abuse, Punishment, and Torture: The Presidential Directorate for Comprehensive Action against Antipersonnel Mines (DAICMA) reported that antipersonnel mines and IEDs, deployed primarily by the FARC and the ELN, caused 11 deaths and 63 injuries from January 1 through the end of October, including four minors. Members of the Colombian military suffered the majority of injuries. During the year the Joint Improvised Threat Defeat Agency found that the FARC's use of IEDs fell below the number of incidents attributed to the ELN. CERAC reported that as of July 19, 228 days had passed since the last land mine or unexploded ordinance incident involving the FARC.

The army's humanitarian demining brigade cleared more than 18 acres, destroyed 49 IEDs, and destroyed two unexploded munitions through October 2016. Halo Trust continued to engage in demining activities, and from January 1 through July 28 cleared more than 44 acres, destroyed 176 land mines, and destroyed five unexploded munitions. In a pilot project in Santa Helena, where Norwegian People's Aid (NPA) performed nontechnical studies and the army's brigade performed land clearance, the organizations cleared more than five acres, destroyed 19 land mines, and destroyed one unexploded munition. In addition the four humanitarian demining NGOs accredited to operate in the country during the year began work in Vista Hermosa, Meta Department.

More broadly, during the year the government strengthened the oversight role of its civilian-led demining authority, DAICMA, and showcased a five-year strategy to become mine-free at the Forum of Experts in May. The plan includes targeting high-risk municipalities, establishing immediate action areas, and developing interagency rapid response teams to address the mine removal process. The army began establishing a 5,000-person Humanitarian Demining Brigade to deepen and focus military capacity for demining. In addition four NGOs supported humanitarian demining: Halo Trust, Handicap International, NPA, and the Colombian Campaign Against Mines.

There were numerous reports that ELN guerrillas mistreated civilians and prisoners, including injured and sick persons.

International organizations reported that systemic sexual violence against women and girls by some armed actors persisted (see section 6, Women). Human rights NGOs Sisma Mujer, Amnesty International, and others reported that sexual violence remained one of the main tools used by illegal armed groups to instill fear and force displacement. The government continued to employ an interagency investigative unit in Bogota, the Elite Sexual Assault Investigative Unit (GEDES), which was dedicated to the investigation of sexual assault cases (see section 6, Women).

Child Soldiers: The ELN routinely engaged in forced recruitment of persons under age 18. According to the United Nations, illegal armed groups killed or threatened children with death on suspicion of being informants for the military. The Colombian Family Welfare Institute (ICBF) estimated the average age of recruitment was 12 years. Having admitted to a practice of recruiting minors in the context of the peace talks, the FARC announced February 9 that it would stop recruiting all minors under the age of 18. On May 15, the government and the FARC issued a joint communique announcing the FARC would release all children under age 15 within its ranks and develop a process for the release of all minors under 18. On September 10, media reported the FARC released 13 minors to the ICRC.

The ICBF stated that it was impossible to know how many FARC child soldiers existed but reported that more than 6,027 children were demobilized from illegal armed groups between 1999 and July 2016. Of the children demobilized through July, 10 percent were of indigenous descent, and 7 percent were Afro-Colombian. During the year through July, 451 children were demobilized. The FARC and other illegal armed groups reportedly used children as combatants and recruiters of other children to act as spies, gather intelligence, cultivate narcotics, and provide logistical support. The children were also reportedly exploited in sex trafficking.

The ICBF provided demobilized children extensive assistance, including education, health care, and psychological support. The ICBF continued its educational outreach program, which included a component on prevention of forced recruitment by illegal armed groups. The program maintained teen and preteen clubs and other avenues for educational outreach in all departments of the country.

The Interagency Committee for the Prevention of the Recruitment and Use of Children by Illegal Armed Groups continued activities to prevent recruitment, use, and sexual violence against children. The committee supported cases in the Attorney General's Office and constructed a communication strategy with a focus on the rights of children and guidelines for the prevention of sexual violence. The committee also formed immediate action teams in several departments. The Attorney General's Office prioritized key cases for processing under the JPL. Cases in which former paramilitary forces were accused of recruiting child soldiers were included in the prioritized cases.

Under the criminal code, the penalty for leaders of armed groups who use child soldiers is six to 10 years' imprisonment and a fine of 600 to 1,000 times the minimum wage.

International organizations continued to identify recruitment of indigenous youth by illegal armed groups as a serious concern.

Also see the Department of State's *Trafficking in Persons Report* at www.state.gov/j/tip/rls/tiprpt/.

Other Conflict-related Abuse: Guerrilla groups and organized criminal groups prevented or limited the delivery of food and medicines to towns and regions in contested drug-trafficking corridors, including efforts of international relief and humanitarian organizations. These actions strained local economies and increased forced displacement. The ELN bombed the Cano Limon-Covenas oil pipeline in Boyaca Department on February 9 and damaged infrastructure, including oil pipelines and energy transmission towers, on February 15. Oil spills resulting from these attacks on oil pipelines also resulted in substantial environmental damage, including harming fish and wildlife, and contaminating rivers and aqueducts carrying potable water. The ELN also held an armed strike in which they threatened anyone who went to work or left their homes in Arauca, Norte de Santander, Casanare, Boyaca, Choco, Cauca, and Bajo Cauca regions on February 14-17, and another in Arauca, Boyaca, Casanare, Santander, Norte de Santander, and Vichada Departments in September. ELN attacks on security forces, energy infrastructure, and civilians continued sporadically through May and June.

The Gulf Clan held an armed strike March 31 in Antioquia, Choco, Sucre, Cordoba, and Cesar Departments that paralyzed transportation and commerce, forced school closures, and led to violence, including the deaths of three police members and one army official.

Guerrillas routinely used civilians to shield combatant forces and forcibly displaced peasants to clear key drug and weapon transit routes in strategic zones. Guerrillas also imposed de facto blockades of communities in regions where they had significant influence. For example, international organizations reported many incidents in which illegal armed groups forcibly recruited indigenous persons or forced them to collaborate, restricted their freedom of movement, and blockaded their communities. The UN Permanent Forum on Indigenous Issues received reports of rape, forced recruitment, use of minors as informants, and other abuses in the context of conflict.

Organized criminal gangs, as well as illegal armed groups, such as ELN guerrillas, forcibly entered private homes, monitored private communications, and engaged in forced displacement and conscription. Organized criminal groups also continued to displace civilians residing along key drug and weapon transit corridors (see section 2.d.).

There were reports that the FARC, the ELN, and other armed actors engaged in the extraction of, and cross-border trade in, conflict minerals, which contributed to abuses by providing funding for weapons and by prompting rebels to displace residents forcibly in order to clear mining areas.

As a confidence-building measure for the peace process, the FARC announced on July 4 an immediate suspension of the levying of extortion "taxes" on civilians engaged in legal economic activity.

Section 2. Respect for Civil Liberties, Including:

a. Freedom of Speech and Press

The law provides for freedom of speech and press, and the government generally respected these rights. Violence and harassment, as well as the criminalization of libel, inhibited freedom of the press, and the government frequently influenced the press, in part through its large advertising budgets. The independent media were active and expressed a wide variety of views without restriction.

<u>Violence and Harassment</u>: According to the domestic NGO Foundation for Press Freedom (FLIP), during the year through August 29, there were 144 incidents of violence and harassment against journalists, although FLIP noted many other incidents might have gone unreported in the most dangerous areas of the country. FLIP reported 52 threats, some aimed simultaneously at more than one journalist. FLIP also reported that one journalist was detained, 33 journalists were physically attacked, and 17 were stigmatized due to their work; however, no journalists had been killed as of September. According to FLIP, the government did not bring a single case to trial for violence against journalists, although investigations continued.

As of July the Human Rights Unit of the Attorney General's Office was investigating 37 active cases of crimes against journalists and had convicted 43 persons for such crimes.

On May 21, the ELN kidnapped RCN journalists Salud Hernandez, Diego D'Pablos, and Carlos Melo. They were released on May 27.

The investigation into the case of journalist Flor Alba Nunez Vargas, shot and killed in 2015, proceeded despite some delays. The accused material author of the crime, Juan Camilo Ortiz, arrested in September 2015, remained in detention, while Ortiz's alleged accomplice, Jaumeth Albeiro Florez, known by the alias "Chori," remained at large. After the preliminary hearing was suspended three times, the prosecution in a September 2 preliminary hearing presented evidence against Ortiz, including 93 elements of proof and legal evidence. The preliminary hearing was suspended again and resumed September 19, according to media reports. Oral proceedings in the case were scheduled for November.

On May 10, the Attorney General's Office called three former DAS employees-- former DAS director in Antioquia Emiro Rojas Granados, existing CTI telematics director William Alberto Merchan, and former DAS intelligence group detective Juan Carlos Sastoque--to testify in the case regarding threats and harassment against journalist Claudia Julieta Duque.

In September the Council of the State, the highest court for legal processes involving the state, ruled the state was responsible for the death of Jaime Garzon, a journalist and satirist shot and killed by motorcycle gunmen in Bogota in 1999. The court sentenced the state, represented by the Ministry of Defense, the army, and the National Police, noting the responsibility of DAS agents. According to the Council of the State, Jose Miguel Narvaez, the former deputy director of intelligence of the DAS, and the former chief of intelligence of Brigade 13 of the army, colonel Jorge Eliecer Plazas Acevedo, carried out illegal wiretaps on Garzon and shared the information with the former commander of the AUC, Carlos Castano, to whom they suggested the murder. The court ordered the state to pay more than COP 700 million ($235,000) to Garzon's family for damages. Plazas Acevedo and Narvaez were being prosecuted for the crime of aggravated homicide. There was only one conviction to date in Garzon's murder; in 2004 Carlos Castano was convicted in absentia of being the mastermind of the murder, and sentenced to 38 years in prison.

As of July the National Protection Unit (NPU) provided protection services to 132 journalists. On September 23, the NPU presented a new Protocol for Attention to Cases of Journalists and/or Social Communicators, established with the stated goal of meeting the particular needs of this group and providing more robust risk studies.

Censorship or Content Restrictions: FLIP alleged that some journalists practiced self-censorship due to fear of being sued under libel laws or of being physically attacked, mostly by nongovernment actors. FLIP argued that the high degree of impunity for those who committed aggressions against journalists was also a factor.

Libel/Slander Laws: By law slander and libel are crimes. There is no specific legislation for slander against public officials. The government did not use prosecution to prevent media from criticizing government policies or public officials. Political candidates, businesspersons, and others, however, sued journalists for expressing their opinions, alleging defamation or libel. FLIP reported three new cases against journalists for libel or slander were filed from January 1 to August 26. FLIP also noted as of August 26, four cases of journalists being prosecuted for libel or slander continued from previous years.

Nongovernmental Impact: Members of illegal armed groups sought to inhibit freedom of expression by intimidating, threatening, kidnapping, and killing journalists. National and international NGOs reported that local media representatives regularly practiced self-censorship because of threats of violence from these groups.

In March a judge sentenced Mario Jaime Mejia to 28 years and Alejandro Cardenas to 11 years in prison for their roles in the aggravated kidnapping, torture, and rape of journalist Jineth Bedoya in 2000. In August the Superior Court of

Bogota ruled that neither man was eligible for the alternative benefits provided by the Justice and Peace law because they lied about their participation in and knowledge of the facts in the case.

Internet Freedom

The government did not restrict or disrupt access to the internet and has no onerous legislation or policies censoring online content.

The investigation continued into past abuses by the Army Intelligence Unit known as "Andromeda" (see also section 1.f.).

The International Telecommunication Union estimated 53 percent of the population used the internet in 2015. In view of the general climate of violence and impunity, self-censorship occurred both online and offline, particularly within communities at risk in rural areas.

Academic Freedom and Cultural Events

There were no government restrictions on academic freedom or cultural events. There was evidence, however, that guerrillas maintained a presence on many university campuses to generate political support for their respective causes and undermine support for their enemies through both violent and nonviolent means.

Organized criminal gangs and guerrilla groups killed, threatened, and displaced educators and their families for political and financial reasons, often because teachers represented the only government presence in the remote areas where the killings occurred.

According to the Colombian Federation of Educators, three educators were killed during the year through August 29. Threats and harassment caused many educators and students to adopt lower profiles and avoid discussing controversial topics.

b. Freedom of Peaceful Assembly and Association

Freedom of Assembly

The law provides for the freedom of assembly, and the government generally respected this right.

Freedom of Association

The law provides for the freedom of association, and the government generally respected this right. Freedom of association was limited by threats and acts of violence committed by illegal armed groups against NGOs, indigenous groups, and labor unions (see section 1.g.). Some NGOs alleged that riot police used excessive force to break up demonstrations. During a two-week national agrarian strike that began May 30 and concluded with the signing of an accord with the government June 12, local social and human rights organizations accused the armed forces and National Police Anti-Riot Squad of using excessive force and alleged that at least 179 demonstrators were injured and three killed. The government stated the protests had not remained peaceful and noted 54 members of the security forces were also injured.

Although the government does not prohibit membership in most political organizations, membership in organizations that engaged in rebellion against the government, espoused violence, or carried out acts of violence, such as the FARC, the ELN, and illegal armed groups, was illegal.

c. Freedom of Religion

See the Department of State's *International Religious Freedom Report* at www.state.gov/religiousfreedomreport/.

d. Freedom of Movement, Internally Displaced Persons, Protection of Refugees, and Stateless Persons

The law provides for freedom of internal movement, foreign travel, emigration, and repatriation. The government generally respected these rights, although there were exceptions. Military operations and armed conflict in certain rural areas restricted freedom of movement.

The government cooperated with the Office of the UN High Commissioner for Refugees (UNHCR) and other humanitarian organizations in providing protection and assistance to internally displaced persons (IDPs), refugees, returning refugees, asylum seekers, stateless persons, and other persons of concern.

In-country Movement: There were no government restrictions on movement within the country. Organized criminal gangs and ELN guerrillas continued to establish illegal checkpoints on rural roads, particularly in the departments of Putumayo, Arauca, Antioquia, and Norte de Santander.

International organizations also reported that illegal armed groups confined rural communities through roadblocks, curfews, car bombs at egress routes, and IEDs in areas where narcotics cultivation and trafficking persisted. According to the UN Office for the Coordination of Humanitarian Affairs, monitoring in the departments where it operated, between January 2015 and August 15, 2016, more than 5.35 million persons faced mobility restrictions that limited their access to essential goods and services due to armed incidents, protests, and geographical factors. The departments most affected were Cordoba, Caqueta, Cauca, and Narino. Of the more than five million persons in those areas, 4.1 million suffered mobility restrictions due to events related to armed violence. The restrictions were generally limited in duration.

On April 1, the Gulf Clan illegal armed group conducted an armed strike in 36 municipalities, killing five persons, blocking five roads, and burning eight trucks. CERAC reported that while four of the killings targeted members of the CNP and army, the majority of the strike activities targeted the civilian population.

Exile: The law prohibits forced exile, and the government did not employ it. Historically, many persons went into self-imposed exile because of threats from organized criminal gangs and FARC and ELN guerrillas.

Internally Displaced Persons

The armed conflict, especially in remote areas, was the major cause of internal displacement. The government, international organizations, and civil society identified various factors driving displacement, including threats, extortion, and physical, psychological, and sexual violence by illegal armed groups against civilian populations, particularly women and girls. Competition and armed confrontation between and within illegal armed groups for resources and territorial control and confrontations between security forces, guerrillas, and organized criminal gangs, and forced recruitment of children or threats of forced recruitment were also drivers of displacement. Some NGOs asserted that counternarcotics efforts, illegal mining, and large-scale commercial ventures in rural areas also contributed to displacement.

The NGO Consultancy for Human Rights and Displacement (CODHES) reported 8,669 persons displaced in mass displacement events (displacement of 50 or more persons) from January through August and indicated the departments with the highest numbers of IDPs from mass displacements in the year were Choco (5,407 displacements), Antioquia (1,250 displacements), Norte de Santander (923 displacements), and Narino (347 displacements). CODHES also reported that eight land-rights leaders were killed from January 1 through August, one land-rights claimant and two employees of the land restitution unit were killed, 10 land rights leaders received individual or collective threats, and eight members of a land rights and human rights organizations were threatened.

As of July the NPU was providing protection services to 300 land restitution leaders.

As of August 1, the government reported the Victims' Unit listed 6,883,513 displaced in the Single Victims Registry, with registrants dating back since 1985. Of those, 17,976 were due to displacements that occurred during the year. Victims' Unit statistics showed that new displacements occurred primarily in areas where narcotics cultivation and trafficking persisted, especially where guerrilla groups and organized criminal gangs were present.

The Victims' Unit maintained the Single Victims Registry as mandated by law. Despite improvements in the government registration system, IDPs experienced delays in receiving responses to their displacement claims because of a large backlog of claims built up during several months. International organizations and NGOs remained concerned about the slow and insufficient institutional response to displacement. Government policy provides for an appeals process in the case of refusals.

The ELN and organized criminal gangs continued to use force, intimidation, and disinformation to discourage IDPs from registering with the government. Guerrilla agents sometimes forced local leaders and community members to demonstrate against government efforts to eradicate illicit crops and forced communities to displace as a form of coerced protest against eradication. International organizations and civil society expressed concern over urban displacement caused by violence stemming from territorial disputes between criminal gangs, some of which had links to larger criminal and narcotics trafficking groups.

The Victims' Unit cited extortion, recruitment by illegal armed groups, homicides, and physical and sexual violence as the primary causes of intra-urban displacement. The ICRC and UNHCR reported that in some departments displacement disproportionately affected indigenous and Afro-Colombian groups.

Through August 1, the government registered 171,634 IDPs (including those displaced during years before 2014) who identified themselves as indigenous and 698,642 who identified themselves as Afro-Colombian. Of those displaced in 2016, 1,025 persons self-identified as indigenous and 2,869 self-identified as Afro-Colombian.

The National Indigenous Organization of Colombia estimated the number of displaced indigenous persons to be much higher than indicated by government reports, since many indigenous persons did not have adequate access to registration locations due to geographic remoteness, language barriers, or unfamiliarity with the national registration system.

The local NGO Association of Internally Displaced Afro-Colombians (AFRODES) stated that threats and violence against Afro-Colombian leaders and communities continued to cause high levels of forced displacement, especially in the Pacific Coast region. AFRODES and other local NGOs repeatedly expressed concern that large-scale economic projects, such as agriculture and mining, contributed to displacement in their communities.

Fifty-two government agencies are responsible by law for assisting registered IDPs. International organizations and NGOs maintained that the quality of programs providing emergency assistance, housing, and income generation need strengthening. Emergency response capacity at the local level was weak, and IDPs continued to experience prolonged periods of vulnerability while waiting for assistance.

A specialized unit of the Attorney General's Office--established through an agreement with the government's former social agency, Social Action (which the DPS replaced), the Attorney General's Office, and the CNP--investigated and prosecuted cases of forced displacement and disappearances.

Dozens of international organizations, international NGOs, and domestic nonprofit groups, including UNHCR, the International Organization for Migration, the World Food Program, the ICRC, and the Colombian Red Cross, coordinated with the government to provide emergency relief and long-term assistance to displaced populations.

The Victims' Unit and other government agencies improved their response to mass displacement events throughout the year and were assisted by international organizations such as UNHCR and the ICRC. International organizations and civil society reported that a continuing lack of local capacity to accept registrations in high-displacement areas often delayed by several weeks or months assistance to persons displaced individually or in smaller groups. Humanitarian organizations attributed the delays to a variety of factors, including the lack of personnel, funding, declaration forms, and training. Intense fighting and insecurity in conflict zones, including areas in the departments of Antioquia, Cauca, Choco, and Narino, sometimes delayed national and international aid organizations from reaching newly displaced populations.

Despite several government initiatives to enhance IDP access to services and awareness of their rights, in many parts of the country, municipalities did not have the resources or capacity to respond to new displacements and provide humanitarian assistance to IDPs. Local elections in October 2015 resulted in new mayors and municipal officials, many of whom were inexperienced in displacement issues. Many IDPs continued to live in poverty in unhygienic conditions and with limited access to health care, education, and employment.

Displaced persons also sought protection across international borders due to the internal armed conflict. UNHCR stated that Colombia was the country of origin for 360,000 refugees and persons in a refugee-like situation, the majority in Ecuador, Venezuela, Costa Rica, and Panama. UNHCR estimated that between 400 and 500 Colombians crossed into Ecuador every month. The governments of Colombia and Ecuador continued to meet throughout the year regarding the situation of Colombian refugees in Ecuador, and the Colombian government offered a program to assist Colombian refugees in Ecuador who returned to Colombia.

Protection of Refugees

<u>Access to Asylum</u>: The law provides for the granting of asylum or refugee status, and the government has established a system for providing protection to refugees. According to the government, it approved 77 of the 1,263 applications for refugee status received since 2009. Between January 1 and August 19, the government reported it received 334 new applications for refugee status, of which it approved eight and rejected 55. As of August 19, the government reported it had not received any complaints of discrimination against the civil rights of refugees.

The government reported a continuing rise in the smuggling of migrants from outside the region through Colombia en route to the United States and Canada. According to UNHCR and Colombian migration officials, most of the undocumented migrants were Cubans and Haitians, followed by Africans and Asians, and most entered through Ecuador, Venezuela, and Brazil. While the government generally provided access to the asylum process for such persons who requested international protection, many abandoned their applications and continued on the migration route.

Section 3. Freedom to Participate in the Political Process

The law provides citizens the ability to choose their government through free and fair periodic elections held by secret ballot and based on nearly universal suffrage. Active-duty members of the armed forces and police may neither vote nor participate in the political process. Civilian public employees are eligible to vote, although they may participate in partisan politics only during the four months immediately preceding a national election.

As part of the peace accord announced on August 24, the government and the FARC agreed to take steps formally to register former FARC members as a political party or political movement after the FARC fully disarm. These features were maintained in the revised accord announced November 12 and approved by the Colombian congress November 30. The revised accord included guaranteed seats for FARC representatives in the Senate and House of Representatives in the 2018 and 2022 elections. It also included security guarantees for the new political party or political movement, guaranteed state financing for the new party or movement's 2018 and 2022 Senate and presidential campaigns, and guarantees regarding access to media under the same conditions as other political parties and movements.

Elections and Political Participation

Recent Elections: In 2015 the country held departmental and local elections, involving 110,000 candidates running to be one of the country's 32 governors, 1,100 mayors, and more than 12,000 local council-seat holders. According to the NGO Foundation of Peace and Reconciliation, during the election period, seven candidates were killed, four were attacked, and 28 were threatened. In October the country voted in a national plebiscite on the peace accord announced by the government and FARC in a contest both the Foundation of Peace and Reconciliation and the Electoral Observation Mission (MOE) reported was generally free, fair, and violence free.

According to MOE, electoral fraud remained a serious concern. The NGO reported that parties paid voters to register and vote in municipalities in which they were not resident. In advance of the 2015 elections, NGOs estimated this occurred in more than 600 municipalities. According to the Foundation of Peace and Reconciliation, the areas with the highest proportion of irregular voters were the departments of Boyaca, Antioquia, Cundinamarca, Narino, and Bolivar. The government continued the use of a new finance tool to provide transparency of campaign funds, disqualified candidates with pending criminal investigations, and canceled the national identification cards of voters who could not demonstrate residence or employment in the municipality where they were registered to vote. The Foundation of Peace and Reconciliation claimed 11 parties' rosters for elections included candidates with financial ties to illegal groups.

Former La Guajira governor Juan Francisco "Kiko" Gomez Cerchar was tried for his alleged involvement in death threats made in 2014 against four persons investigating political party corruption and ties to illegal armed groups, for links to former paramilitary groups, and for involvement in various killings. On November 17, he was convicted of crimes including aggravated homicide, attempted murder, and trafficking of weapons in connection with the killings of political leader Yandra Brito, her husband Henry Ustariz, and driver Wilfredo Fonseca.

Political Parties and Political Participation: Organized criminal gangs and the ELN threatened and killed government officials (see section 1.g.). Some local officials resigned because of threats from the FARC. As of August 22, the NPU, under the Ministry of Interior, provided protection to 282 mayors, 22 governors, and 2,581 other persons, including members of departmental assemblies, council members, judges, municipal human rights officers, and other officials related to national human rights policies. By decree the CNP's protection program and the NPU assume shared responsibility for protecting municipal and district mayors.

Participation of Women and Minorities: No laws limit participation of women and members of minorities in the political process, and they did participate. During the 2014 legislative elections, two persons who were allegedly not of Afro-Colombian descent, Maria del Socorro Bustamante and Moises Orozco Vicuna, were elected to the two seats in the House of Representatives reserved for representatives of Afro-Colombian communities. Legal challenges following the election kept the individuals from assuming their seats. One of the candidates, Bustamante, died of natural causes in 2015. In October the Superior Court of Cundinamarca validated the appointment of Heriberto Arrechea to fill Orozco Vicuna's seat.

The number of women elected to public office increased in general in the October 2015 elections, according to UN Women's 2014-15 report. As a result of the elections, the percentage of women holding local public office rose from 13 percent to 15.5 percent. Five of 32 elected governors and 133 of 1,109 mayors were women. Additionally, women constitute 20 percent of the House of Representatives and 23 percent of the Senate, compared with 12.7 percent of the House and 16.7 percent of the Senate in 2010. In the plenary chamber of the Supreme Court of Justice, three of the 22 justices were women.

Section 4. Corruption and Lack of Transparency in Government

The law provides criminal penalties for official corruption, and the government generally implemented these laws effectively, although officials sometimes engaged in corrupt practices without punishment. The World Bank's worldwide governance indicators reflected that government corruption was a serious problem. Revenues from transnational organized crime, including drug trafficking, exacerbated corruption.

Corruption: In January media reported 12 persons were arrested for alleged corruption related to ICBF contracts, including the former ICBF regional director in Barranquilla Department and an active CNP officer. According to media reporting, an estimated COP 1.755 trillion ($600 million) was embezzled. Additionally, two ICBF officials were arrested in August for their alleged involvement in a corruption scandal related to contracts worth millions of dollars for the care of minors and pregnant women within the ICBF's "Cero a Siempre" strategy. The two officials faced charges for crimes, including embezzlement, procedural fraud, forgery of private documents, falsifying a public document, and malfeasance.

A special investigative unit of the Supreme Court of Justice, charged with investigating members of congress and senior government officials, reported that since January 1, it opened one investigation against a former senator; the investigation. During the same period, the unit opened 59 investigations against former governors and 28 against sitting governors but won no convictions in the cases.

The Attorney General's Office reported that for the year through September, it had investigated 19 attorneys, one comptroller, and 16 other senior government officials. In addition, as of August 25, the Attorney General's Office was investigating 75 cases of corruption, of which 71 were in the preliminary investigation phase and four had been brought to trial.

Financial Disclosure: By law public officials must file annual financial disclosure forms with the tax authority. The information is not made public. The law states that persons who intend to hold public office or work as contractors for the government for more than three months shall submit a statement of assets and income, as well as information on their private economic activity. The Administrative Department of Public Service is in charge of preparing the required forms, and the human resources chief in each entity is responsible for verifying the information submitted. Congress maintained a website on which members could voluntarily post their financial information.

Public Access to Information: The law provides for public access to government information, and the government generally provided this access. There were reports that some low-level officials insisted on bribes to expedite access to information.

Section 5. Governmental Attitude Regarding International and Nongovernmental Investigation of Alleged Violations of Human Rights

A wide variety of domestic and international human rights groups generally operated without government restriction, investigating and publishing their findings on human rights cases. Although the government and local human rights groups often differed in their evaluations and analyses of the human rights situation, government officials were typically cooperative and willing to listen to the groups' concerns.

International NGOs and institutions warned of possible increased violence against civil society leaders and human rights defenders and its potential to undermine peace accord implementation. According to the NGO Somos Defensores (We Are Defenders), 35 human rights activists were killed and 279 threatened, arbitrarily detained, robbed, or disappeared during the first half of the year. Of the killings, 85 percent were committed by hired killers, while 84 percent of the threats were attributable to former paramilitary groups and 13 percent to organized crime, with the rest unknown. Somos Defensores reported that the departments most affected by the attacks were Cauca, Antioquia, Valle de Cauca, Norte de Santander, and Cundinamarca.

The minister of interior continued to make public statements in support of human rights defenders and called on the Attorney General's Office to investigate crimes committed against them. In 2015 the Attorney General's Office issued Resolutions 249 and 1783 to investigate cybercrimes, threats, and violence committed against human rights defenders.

Somos Defensores reported that in the cases of human rights defenders killed in 2015 and the first six months of 2016, eight cases were in the sentencing stage and eight were in the trial stage as of June.

Several NGOs reported receiving threats in the form of e-mails, mail, telephone calls, false obituaries, and objects related to death, such as coffins and funeral bouquets. The government condemned the threats and called on the Attorney General's Office to investigate them. Some activists claimed the government did not take the threats seriously.

Through July 31, the Attorney General's Office reported 663 active investigations and no convictions in cases of threats against human rights defenders.

As of June the NPU's protection program provided protection to a total of 6,198 individuals. Among the NPU's protected persons were 478 human rights activists.

Government Human Rights Bodies: The ombudsman is independent, submits an annual report to the House of Representatives, and has responsibility for providing for the promotion and exercise of human rights. Ombudsman Jorge Armando Otalora resigned on January 27 due to labor and sexual harassment allegations. The new ombudsman, Carlos Alfonso Negret Mosquera, was elected on August 16 for the period of September 2016 through August 2020. According to human rights groups, underfunding of the Ombudsman's Office limited its ability to monitor violations effectively. Members of the ombudsman's regional offices reported threats from illegal armed groups through pamphlets, e-mails, and violent actions.

The National System for Human Rights and International Humanitarian Law--led by a commission of 11 senior government officials coordinates and the vice president--designs, implements, and evaluates the government's human rights and international humanitarian law policies. The Office of the Presidential Advisor for Human Rights coordinates national human rights policy and actions taken by government entities to promote or protect human rights. The program publishes regional, national, and thematic reports on human rights topics. The program continued to host public forums with civil society groups, local and national government groups, and the international community. The program continued to advocate for implementation of the public policy recommendations from 32 regional forums conducted in 2012 and 2013.

Both the Senate and House of Representatives had human rights committees that served as forums for discussion of human rights problems.

Section 6. Discrimination, Societal Abuses, and Trafficking in Persons

Women

<u>Rape and Domestic Violence</u>: Although prohibited by law, rape, including spousal rape, remained a serious problem. The law provides for sentences ranging from eight to 30 years' imprisonment for violent sexual assault. For acts of spousal sexual violence, the law mandates prison sentences of six months to two years and denies probation or bail to offenders who disobey restraining orders. By law femicide is punishable with penalties of 21 to 50 years in prison, without the possibility of suspensions or reductions, and longer than the minimum sentence of 13 years for homicide. Femicide is defined as the killing of a woman either for being a woman, because of her gender identity, or as a part of a cycle of sexual, physical, or psychological violence.

There was no comprehensive or consolidated database on the incidence of sexual violence, but NGO groups claimed that rape continued to be underreported. The Attorney General's Office indicated that many cases went unreported. Members of illegal groups, including former paramilitary members, and guerrillas also continued to rape and abuse women and children sexually.

Prosecution rates for rape continued to be low. Women's groups, such as Sisma Mujer, assessed the extent of rape and domestic violence to be widespread and the law enforcement response to be generally ineffective. The Attorney General's Office had teams in each of its 35 regional directorates that specialize in providing technical assistance and other support in cases of sexual violence, including sexual violence within the context of the internal armed conflict. The government continued to employ the GEDES interagency unit in Bogota, which is dedicated to the investigation of sexual assault cases. The unit uses a multidisciplinary task force approach that includes prosecutors, investigators, and forensic specialists from the CNP and the Attorney General's Office, working together under a common investigative and prosecutorial model. Through the end of August, the

Attorney General's Office opened 21,848 investigations for sexual abuses. The Attorney General's Office reported that between January and the end of July, there were 56 new convictions obtained for sexual abuse, including sexual assault, with 12,841 more cases in the trial stage. In addition, during the year through July, the Inspector General's Office reported no open disciplinary investigations into members of the security forces for sex crimes.

Through July the Attorney General's Office reported 62,186 new investigations had been opened for cases of domestic violence. Of the victims, 53,596 of the victims were women, and 2,607 of the cases involved minors.

The law allows authorities to prosecute domestic violence offenders when the victim does not testify, if there is another witness. Judicial authorities may remove an abuser from a household and require the abuser to undergo therapy. The law provides for both fines and prison time if an abuser causes grave harm or the abuse is recurrent, but authorities reportedly did not impose fines.

The law requires the government to provide victims of domestic violence immediate protection from further physical or psychological abuse. The ICBF provided safe houses and counseling for some women and children who were victims of domestic violence, but its services could not meet total demand. In addition to fulfilling traditional family counseling functions, the ICBF family ombudsmen handled domestic violence cases.

The Ministry of Defense continued implementing its protocol for managing cases of sexual violence and harassment involving members of the military.

The law augments both jail time and fines if the crime causes "transitory or permanent physical disfigurement," such as acid attacks, in which an attacker throws acid onto the victim's face. A law passed on January 6 defines acid attacks as a specific crime, punishing the possession, manufacturing, and trafficking of dangerous substances with prison sentences of 12.5 to 40 years and a wage-based fine. The law also stipulates that the National Institute of Legal Medicine must provide hospitals with training on care for acid-attack victims. In Bogota on August 9, Maria Helena Pena, a 50-year-old female acid-attack victim, had only 5 percent of her face damaged because of the quick action of informed neighbors and hospital workers. In 2014, also in Bogota, Natalia Ponce de Leon was the victim of an acid attack that caused serious burns to her face and body. In August the courts upheld her attacker's conviction and sentence of 20-25 years in prison and rejected the attacker's insanity defense.

<u>Female Genital Mutilation/Cutting (FGM/C)</u>: The law prohibits FGM/C, but isolated incidents were reported in several indigenous communities. No accurate statistics existed regarding the practice, which generally includes types I and IV, according to the World Health Organization's classification system.

Government efforts to prevent FGM/C included achieving in 2011 a continuing commitment from the sizable Embera-Chami indigenous group to renounce the practice. The tribe's commitment continued, but on March 3, according to media reports, two indigenous children, each under one month old, of the Embera-Chami community of Antioquia died after an ablation surgery.

The UN Population Fund continued to support a consulting project on FGM/C with indigenous peoples. The project's goal is to eradicate practices harmful to the life and health of indigenous girls and women nationwide, with an emphasis on the departments of Risaralda and Choco.

<u>Sexual Harassment</u>: The law provides measures to deter and punish harassment in the workplace, such as sexual harassment, verbal abuse or derision, aggression, and discrimination. Nonetheless, NGOs reported that sexual harassment remained a pervasive and underreported problem. No information was available as to whether the government implemented the law effectively.

<u>Reproductive Rights</u>: Couples and individuals have the right to decide the number, spacing, and timing of children; manage their reproductive health; and have access to the information and means to do so, free from discrimination, coercion, and violence.

During the year there were reports of forced abortions. Through July 31, the Attorney General's Office reported it opened 20 investigations related to cases of forced abortion, 18 of which had occurred during the year.

<u>Discrimination</u>: Although women enjoy the same legal rights as men, serious discrimination against women persisted (see section 7.d.).

The Office of the Advisor for the Equality of Women has primary responsibility for combating discrimination against women, but advocacy groups reported that the office remained seriously underfunded. The government continued its national public policy for gender equity. The policy includes directives for affording women access to economic autonomy, decision-making positions, health and reproductive rights, and a life free of violence, as well as incorporating a gender focus into education.

Children

Birth Registration: Citizenship is derived by birth within the country's territory. Most births were registered immediately. If a birth is not registered within one month, parents may be fined and denied public services.

Child Abuse: Child abuse was a serious problem. The ICBF reported 6,024 cases of child abuse and 5,643 cases of sexual abuse against children during the year through July 31. Through July 30, ICBF reported it provided assistance, including legal and psychological support, to 5,885 minors who were victims of sexual violence, including cases of sexual exploitation. The Attorney General's Office reported that 91 percent of the investigations it opened during the year involving sexual abuse of minors involved children under age 14 (the minimum age of consent).

A two-year investigation carried out by the Attorney General's Office and concluded during the year documented 214 cases of girls who were subjected to rape, forced sterilization, forced abortion, and other forms of sexual violence by the FARC. According to then acting attorney general Perdomo, the results revealed the FARC instituted a policy of sexual violence against women at least since 1997.

Early and Forced Marriage: Marriage is legal at age 18. Boys older than 14 and girls more than 12 may marry with the consent of their parents.

Female Genital Mutilation/Cutting (FGM/C): See information for girls under 18 in women's section above.

Sexual Exploitation of Children: Sexual exploitation of children remained a problem. The law defines demand for the sexual exploitation of a minor as "directly or through a third party requesting or demanding performance of carnal or sexual acts with a person under 18 years of age, through payment or promise of payment in cash, kind, or compensation of any nature." Sexual exploitation of a minor or facilitating the sexual exploitation of a minor carries a penalty of 14 to 25 years in prison, with aggravated penalties for perpetrators who are family members of the victim and for cases of sexual tourism, forced marriage, or sexual exploitation by illegal armed groups. The law prohibits pornography using children under age 18 and stipulates a penalty of 10 to 20 years in prison and a fine. The minimum age for consensual sex is 14. The penalty for sexual activity with a child under 14 ranges from nine to 13 years in prison. According to the ICBF, during the year through July 31, there were 206 reported cases of commercial sexual exploitation of children.

Since 2009 the NGO Renacer Foundation certified 278 tourism-related businesses as committed to the fight against the sexual exploitation of children and adolescents. In cooperation with the government, Renacer trained 18,426 employees of these businesses in how to identify and fight sexual exploitation.

Displaced Children: The NGO Consultancy for Human Rights and Displacement estimated that 31 percent of persons registered as displaced since 1985 were minors at the time they were displaced (see also section 2.d., IDPs).

International Child Abductions: The country is a party to the 1980 Hague Convention on the Civil Aspects of International Child Abduction. For information see the Department of State's *Annual Report on International Parental Child Abduction* at travel.state.gov/content/childabduction/en/legal/compliance.html.

Anti-Semitism

The Jewish community, which had an estimated 4,200 members, reported instances of anti-Israel rhetoric that emerged around events in the Middle East and were accompanied by anti-Semitic graffiti near synagogues and demonstrations in front of the Israeli Embassy that were sometimes accompanied by anti-Semitic comments on social media.

Trafficking in Persons

See the Department of State's *Trafficking in Persons Report* at www.state.gov/j/tip/rls/tiprpt/.

Persons with Disabilities

The law prohibits discrimination against persons with physical and mental disabilities but not sensory or intellectual disabilities in employment, education, access to public buildings, air travel and other transportation, access to health care, the judicial system, or the provision of other government services. There is no law mandating access to information and telecommunications for persons with disabilities. A 2015 law strengthened penalties for discrimination against persons with disabilities, race, ethnicity, religion, nationality, political or philosophical ideology, sex or sexual orientation, and other grounds. It punishes those who arbitrarily prevent, obstruct, or restrict the full exercise of the rights of persons with disabilities or harass persons with disabilities.

The Office of the Presidential Advisor for Human Rights under the High Counselor for Post-Conflict, Public Security, and Human Rights, along with the Human Rights Directorate at the Ministry of Interior, is responsible for protecting the rights of persons with disabilities. Somos Defensores and other NGOs claimed these laws were seldom enforced.

Although children with disabilities attended school at all levels, advocates noted the vast majority of teachers and schools were neither trained nor equipped to educate children with disabilities successfully. Advocacy groups also stated children with disabilities entered the education system later than children without disabilities and dropped out at higher rates. Advocates also noted that children with disabilities were more vulnerable to sexual and other forms of abuse and that citizens with disabilities were hampered in their ability to vote and participate in civic affairs due to lack of adequate transportation or adequate access to voting facilities in numerous locations throughout the country. Persons with disabilities were unemployed at a much higher rate than the general population (see section 7.d.).

Forced surgical sterilization of children with cognitive and psychosocial disabilities in certain cases is legal.

In 2013 the State Council ordered all public offices to make facilities accessible to persons with disabilities and asked public officials to include requirements for accessibility when granting licenses for construction and occupancy. The State Council also asked every municipality to enforce rules that would make all public offices accessible to persons with disabilities "in a short amount of time." No information was available on how many public offices and facilities complied with the order and undertook accessibility reconstruction projects during the year.

National/Racial/Ethnic Minorities

According to the most recent (2005) national census, approximately 4.5 million persons, or 10 percent of the country's population, described themselves as being of African descent. A 2011 UN report estimated Afro-Colombians made up 15 to 20 percent of the population, while human rights groups and Afro-Colombian organizations estimated the proportion to be 20 to 25 percent.

Afro-Colombians are entitled to all constitutional rights and protections, but they faced significant economic and social discrimination. According to a 2016 UN report, 32 percent of the country's population lived below the poverty line, but in Choco, the department with the highest percentage of Afro-Colombian residents, 79 percent of residents lived below the poverty line. NGO Afro-Colombian Solidarity Network reported 32 percent of Choco's residents lived in extreme poverty. Choco continued to experience the lowest per capita level of social investment; ranked last among departments in terms of infrastructure, education, and health; and experienced the highest rate of income inequality in the country.

In 2010 the government approved a policy to promote equal opportunity for black, Afro-Colombian, Palenquera, and Raizal populations. (Palenquera populations inhabit some parts of the Caribbean coast, Raizal populations live in the San Andres archipelago, and Blacks and Afro-Colombians are Colombians of African descent who self-identify slightly differently based on their unique linguistic and cultural heritages.) The government's National Development Plan 2014-18 stipulates that the budgetary resources allocated to Afro-Colombian, Palenquera, and Raizal populations be no less than what was assigned in the 2010-14 period. The government's Observatory against Racism and Discrimination continued to monitor the use of specialized approaches in public policies for ethnic minorities, to conduct studies on racism and discrimination, and to make recommendations to other public entities regarding the promotion of equal opportunities. The Ministry of Interior continued to provide technical advice and funding for productive and self-sustaining projects presented by Afro-Colombian communities. The government also continued a working committee on problems of Afro-descendants with other members of the Andean Community of Nations and maintained a binational ethnic affairs committee with Ecuador.

The National Autonomous Congress of Afro-Colombian Community Councils and Ethnic Organizations for Blacks, Afro-Colombians, Raizales, and Palenqueras, consisting of 108 representatives, continued to meet with government representatives on problems that affected their communities. Some Afro-Colombian communities, however, complained that those elected to the National Autonomous Congress did not represent their interests.

Indigenous People

The constitution and law give special recognition to the fundamental rights of indigenous persons, who make up approximately 3.4 percent of the population, and require the government to consult beforehand with indigenous groups regarding governmental actions that could affect them.

The law accords indigenous groups perpetual rights to their ancestral lands, but indigenous groups, neighboring landowners, and the government often disputed the demarcation of those lands. Traditional indigenous groups operated 722 reservations, accounting for approximately 28 percent of the country's territory, with officials selected according to indigenous traditions. Many indigenous communities, however, had no legal title to the lands they claimed, and illegal armed groups often violently contested indigenous land ownership and recruited indigenous children to join their ranks.

The law provides for special criminal and civil jurisdictions within indigenous territories based on traditional community laws. Legal proceedings in these jurisdictions were subject to manipulation and often rendered punishments more lenient than those imposed by regular civilian courts.

Some indigenous groups continued to assert that they were not able to participate adequately in decisions affecting their lands. Indigenous leaders complained of the occasional presence of government security forces on indigenous reservations and asked that the government consult with indigenous authorities prior to taking military action against illegal armed groups operating in or around such areas and before building roads or other public works on or near their lands. The constitution provides for this "prior consultation" mechanism for indigenous communities, but it does not require the government to obtain the consent of those communities in all cases.

The government stated that for security reasons it could not provide advance notice of most military operations, especially when in pursuit of enemy combatants, and added that it consulted with indigenous leaders when possible before entering land held by the communities. The law permits the presence of government security forces on indigenous lands, but defense ministry directives instruct security forces to respect the integrity of indigenous communities, particularly during military and police operations.

Despite special legal protections and government assistance programs, indigenous persons continued to suffer discrimination and often lived on the margins of society. They belonged to the country's poorest population and had the highest age-specific mortality rates. Indigenous women faced triple discrimination on the basis of gender, ethnicity, and lower economic status. As of the end of July, the Attorney General's Office reported there were 75 active investigations of 232 military members and 26 members of the CNP accused of violating the rights, culture, or customs of indigenous groups.

Killings of members and leaders of indigenous groups remained a problem. Four indigenous persons were killed in Narino and Cauca Departments during the weekend of August 26-29. During the year through September 1, the NGO National Indigenous Organization of Colombia reported that 11 indigenous persons were killed.

Acts of Violence, Discrimination, and Other Abuses Based on Sexual Orientation and Gender Identity

There was no official discrimination based on sexual orientation in employment, housing, statelessness, or access to education or health care. An August 2015 Constitutional Court decision required that the Ministry of Education modify its educational materials to address discrimination based on sexual orientation or gender identity in schools. In 2015 the Constitutional Court granted gay couples the right to adopt children and in April 2016 the court granted gay couples the legal right to marry. But in September 2016, the First Committee of the Senate, which hears matters related to constitutional reform, statutory laws, and other topics, approved on first reading a bill proposed by Senator Vivian Morales that seeks to clarify who may and may not adopt children. Senator Morales's proposal would convoke a national referendum on amending Article 44 of the Constitution to specify that only heterosexual couples who are married or have a civil union may adopt a child.

Members of the transgender community cited barriers to public services when health-care providers or police officers refused to accept government-issued identification with transgender individuals' names and photographs. Some transgender individuals complained that it was difficult for them to change the gender designation on national identity documents and that transgender individuals whose identity cards listed them as male were still required to show proof that they had performed mandatory military service or obtained the necessary waivers from that service. NGOs claimed that discrimination and violence in prisons against persons due to their sexual orientation or gender identity remained a problem. In addition there were instances where authorities denied medical services to transgender individuals.

Despite government measures to increase the rights and protection of LGBTI persons, there were reports of societal abuse and discrimination, as well as sexual assault. NGOs claimed that transgender individuals, particularly transgender men, were often sexually assaulted in so-called corrective rape. The Constitutional Court pronounced in August that transgender persons faced discrimination and social rejection within the LGBTI community and recommended measures to increase respect for transgender identities in the classrooms. Specifically, the court recommended prohibiting discrimination based on gender identity in educational environments and increasing training on these issues for the educational community. The court also decreed that the autonomy of schools has constitutional limitations and the National Service of Learning (SENA) must adapt its activities to respect and promote gender identity and sexual orientation.

As of July 31, the Attorney General's Office was investigating at least 346 alleged homicides of LGBTI individuals that occurred since January 1. Colombia Diversa, an NGO focused on addressing violence and discrimination due to sexual orientation, claimed at least 21 killings during the year through September 2 due to prejudice regarding sexual orientation or gender identity. Police arrested two individuals in connection with the killings.

Colombia Diversa also reported 10 cases, involving 15 victims, of police abuse of persons due to their sexual orientation or gender identity, with the majority of complaints coming from transgender individuals. According to NGOs working on LGBTI problems, these attacks occurred frequently, but victims did not pursue cases due to fear of retaliation. NGOs also reported several cases of threats against human rights defenders working on LGBTI issues, including the killing of a transgender activist in June in Riohacha, as well as a high level of impunity for crimes against members of the LGBTI community. Such organizations partially attributed impunity levels to the failure of the Attorney General's Office to distinguish and effectively pursue crimes against the LGBTI community.

The manual of administrative procedures for blood banks issued by the Ministry of Health states that, to protect the recipient of a transfusion from HIV/AIDS, it excludes those donors who had "male homosexual relations in the past 15 years." In 2012 the Constitutional Court ordered the Ministry of Health to remove selection criteria based on the sexual orientation of donors, but the regulation reportedly was not changed as of September.

The Center for Historical Memory released and disseminated a first-of-its-kind report, *Annihilate Differences: LGBTI Populations in the Colombian Armed Conflict*, detailing the effects of the country's internal armed conflict on the LGBTI community.

HIV and AIDS Social Stigma

There were no confirmed reports of societal violence or discrimination against persons with HIV/AIDS. In the most recent demographic and health survey (2010), the government reported the responses of 85 percent of those surveyed indicated discriminatory attitudes towards persons with HIV/AIDS, reflecting low levels of social acceptance throughout the country.

Section 7. Worker Rights

a. Freedom of Association and the Right to Collective Bargaining

The law provides for the right of workers to form and join unions, bargain collectively, and conduct legal strikes, and it prohibits antiunion discrimination. Members of associated workers' cooperatives are not allowed to form unions, since the law recognizes members of a cooperative as owners. The law prohibits members of the armed forces and police from forming or joining unions. The law provides for automatic recognition of unions that obtain 25 signatures from potential members and that comply with a registration process. Public-sector employees legally have the right to bargain collectively. The government and employers generally respected freedom of association and collective bargaining in practice. Workers faced some obstacles to exercising those rights, and the government faced numerous challenges effectively enforcing applicable laws governing those two rights.

The law permits associated workers' cooperatives (CTAs), collective pacts, and union contracts. Under collective pacts employers may negotiate accords on pay and labor conditions with workers in workplaces where no union is present or where a union represents less than one-third of employees. Law and regulations prohibit the use of CTAs and collective pacts to undermine the right to organize and bargain collectively, including by extending better conditions to nonunion workers through such pacts. A company may contract the union, at times formed explicitly for this purpose, for a specific job or work; the union then in essence serves as an employer for its members. Workers who belong to a union that has a union contract with a company do not have a direct employment relationship with either the company or the union. Labor disputes for workers under a union contract may be decided through an arbitration panel versus labor courts if both parties agree.

The law does not permit members of the armed forces, police, and persons performing "essential public services" to strike. Before conducting a strike, unions must follow prescribed legal procedures, including entering into a conversation period with the employer, presenting a list of demands, and gaining majority approval in the union for a strike. The law limits strikes to occur only during periods of contract negotiations or collective bargaining and allows employers to fire trade unionists who participate in strikes or work stoppages determined to be illegal by the courts.

The government has the authority to fine labor-rights violators. The government sought to enforce most applicable labor laws, but a lack of an inspection strategy, as well as an overburdened judicial system, inhibited speedy and consistent application. The maximum penalty for violations of law, including those that prohibit the misuse of CTAs, is 5,000 times the minimum monthly wage or COP 3.4 billion ($1.2 million). The law also stipulates that offenders repeatedly misusing CTAs or other labor relationships shall receive the maximum penalty and may be subject to losing their legal status to operate altogether. Employers who engage in antiunion practices may also be imprisoned for up to five years, although government officials admitted a fine was more likely than imprisonment. Prohibited practices include impeding workers' right legally to strike, meet, or otherwise associate, and extending better conditions to members of collective pacts rather than union members. Through April the government reported seven fines on certain subcontracting entities for abusive forms of subcontracting at a value of COP 2.196 billion ($750,600). During the year SENA, the agency tasked with collecting the fines, subcontracted the administrative process for the collection of fines in an attempt to improve and expedite fine collection.

The Ministry of Labor's Special Investigations Unit continued to exercise its power to investigate and impose sanctions in any jurisdiction. The vice minister for labor relations decides on a case-by-case basis whether to assign the Special Investigations Unit or the regional inspectors to investigate certain sites.

The Ministry of Labor leads a tripartite Inter-Institutional Commission for the Promotion and Protection of the Human Rights of Workers, with participation by the government, organized labor groups, and the business community. The commission has not met since October 2015.

As part of its commitments under the 2011 Colombian Action Plan Related to Labor Rights (Labor Action Plan), the government continued to take steps to protect internationally recognized labor rights. Labor inspections by the Ministry of Labor for abusive subcontracting in the five priority sectors of palm oil, sugar, ports, mines, and cut flowers remained infrequent, however. Critics claimed inspections lacked necessary rigor, assessed fines were not collected, and abusive subcontracting continued. The government continued to engage in regular meetings with unions and civil society groups.

The Ministry of Labor, in collaboration with the International Labor Organization (ILO), continued technical training for labor inspectors on how to identify antiunion conduct via a virtual training program. It also implemented methods, including contract and process maps, as strategic planning tools to prioritize interventions. The ministry continued to employ a telephone- and internet-based complaint mechanism to report alleged labor violations. The government reported the mechanism allowed its personnel to attend to 1.5 million citizens in 2015. Union members complained that existing systems did not allow citizens to register anonymous complaints and noted that complaints registered through the telephone and internet systems do not result in action.

Judicial police, the CTI, and prosecutors investigating criminal cases of threats and killings are required to determine during the initial phase of an investigation whether a victim is an active or retired union member or is actively engaged in union formation and organization, but it was unclear whether they actually did this. It could take several months to transfer cases from regional field offices of the Attorney General's Office to the ministry's Human Rights Directorate, and cases are transferred only with the approval of the attorney general in response to direct requests, instead of automatically.

The government continued to include in its protection program for labor activists persons engaged in efforts to form a union, as well as former unionists under threat because of their past activities. Through July the NPU provided protection to 500 trade union leaders or members (others protected included journalists, human rights advocates, and land restitution claimants). Approximately 11.3 percent of the NPU's budget was dedicated to unionist protection. Between January 1 and

September 30, the NPU processed 151 risk assessments of union leaders or members; 97 of those cases were assessed as posing an "extraordinary threat," and the NPU provided them protection measures. The NPU reported that through March, the average time needed to implement protection measures upon completion of a risk analysis was 15 days in regular cases, or five days for emergency cases. NGOs, however, complained about slow processing times.

The protection and relocation of teachers falls under the Ministry of National Education and the departmental education secretaries, but the NPU retains some responsibilities for the risk analysis and protection of family members. During the year through July 31, the NPU evaluated 63 threat cases against teachers and found 36 to be of extraordinary risk.

In cases of unionist killings from previous years, the pace of investigations and convictions remained slow, and high rates of impunity continued. Labor groups stated more needed to be done to address impunity for perpetrators of violence against trade unionists and the large number of threat cases. The Attorney General's Office indicated it prioritized cases in order of severity and had a backlog of lower-priority cases. As of July 31, the Attorney General's Office reported 966 active cases of violence against unionists in prior years that were lodged in the Human Rights Directorate. Since 2011, there have been 30 convictions in cases of violence against unionists.

Violence, threats, harassment, and other practices against trade unionists continued to affect the exercise of the right to freedom of association and collective bargaining. According to the Colombian Federation of Educators, during the year through August 29, three educators were killed.

The National Union School (ENS), a labor rights NGO and think tank, reported that eight trade unionists were killed during the year through August 10. ENS and other labor groups stated that focusing on killings alone masked the true nature and scope of the violence against labor activists. Labor groups noted that in some regions nonlethal violations continued to increase. The ENS reported during the same period 82 death threats, nine nonlethal attacks, three arbitrary detentions, 16 cases of harassment, and two cases of illegal raids.

Investigations continued into the 2013 killing of the leader of the Sintrainagro labor union, Juan Carlos Perez, and the 2015 murder of Union of Judicial Employees (Asonal) treasurer, Alex Fabian Espinsoa Carvajalino. Perez, who was advocating on behalf of approximately 90 dismissed workers, had received earlier death threats.

Unions cited multiple instances in which companies fired employees who formed or sought to form new unions. Some employers continued to use temporary contracts, service agencies, and other forms of subcontracting to limit worker rights and protections. Fines assessed by the government did little to dissuade violators, since fines were often not collected. In the first eight months of the year, the government reported that 497 workers benefited from 15 formalization agreements that the Ministry of Labor reached with employers in the departments of Amazonas, Barrancabermeja, Caqueta, Casanare, Valle del Cauca, Cesar, Choco, Huila, Norte de Santander, Putumayo, Quindio, and Uraba, as well as in Bogota.

Labor confederations and NGOs reported that some business owners in several sectors used "simplified stock corporations" (SAS), union contracts, foundations, or temporary service agencies in attempts to circumvent legal restrictions on cooperatives. While in theory SAS workers may exercise their right to organize and bargain collectively with SAS management, it appeared that in some cases the SAS had little or no control over the conditions of employment. The Ministry of Labor stated that an SAS, like any corporate structure, may be fined for labor violations if they occurred. In April the government issued a decree on subcontracting. As of August there were two legal challenges to the decree pending.

According to ENS, Indupalma, a large employer in the palm sector located in the municipality of San Alberto, Cesar department, employed more than 1,800 workers through illegal cooperatives. This reportedly was the only company in the region that continued using labor intermediation with illegal cooperatives with no sanctions or corrective measures by the Ministry of Labor.

In August 2015 Las Brisas, the first palm-sector business fined for using illegal cooperatives, paid the fine imposed on it in 2012. As of October, that fine remained the only large-scale fine collected for illegal subcontracting in the Labor Action Plan priority sectors.

Metal and mineworkers' union SINTRAIME reported that inspections for abusive subcontracting carried out by the Ministry of Labor at the Drummond coal mines have been ineffective in safeguarding the freedom of workers to organize.

b. Prohibition of Forced or Compulsory Labor

The law prohibits all forms of forced or compulsory labor. The government did not effectively enforce the law in all cases, and there continued to be some reports that such practices occurred. The law prescribes punishments of 13 to 23 years' imprisonment plus fines for forced labor violations, penalties that are sufficiently stringent.

There were some reports that FARC and ELN guerrillas and organized criminal gangs used forced labor, including forced child labor, in coca cultivation and illegal mining in areas outside government control (see section 1.g.), as well as forced criminal activity in urban areas. The ICBF noted it was difficult to produce exact statistics on the number of children who participated in illegal armed groups due to the groups' clandestine nature. On February 9, the FARC announced that it would stop recruiting children under the age of 18. The FARC reached an agreement with the government on May 15 on how to release minors already in the ranks and facilitate their reintegration. In September the FARC released 13 children to the ICRC.

Forced labor in other sectors, including organized begging, mining, agriculture, forced recruitment by illegal armed actors, and domestic service, also remained a serious problem. Afro-Colombians, indigenous Colombians, and inhabitants of marginalized urban areas were at the highest risk of forced labor, domestic servitude, forced begging, and forced recruitment.

Also see the Department of State's *Trafficking in Persons Report* at www.state.gov/j/tip/rls/tiprpt/.

c. Prohibition of Child Labor and Minimum Age for Employment

The law sets the minimum age for employment at 15 and at 18 for hazardous work. Children 15 and 16 years of age may work no more than 30 hours per week, and children age 17 may work no more than 40 hours per week. Children under 15 may work in arts, sports, or recreational or cultural activities for a maximum of 14 hours per week. In all these cases, working children and adolescents must have signed documentation filed by their parents and approved by a labor inspector or other local authority.

The law prohibits child workers from working at night or where there is a risk of bodily harm or exposure to excessive heat, cold, or noise. Hazardous work includes an extensive list of activities within 11 occupational categories and subcategories identified as the "worst forms of child labor," including agriculture, hunting and forestry, fishing, mining and quarrying, manufacturing, construction, transport and storage, health services, and defense.

The law authorizes inspectors to issue fines of up to 5,000 times the minimum monthly wage for labor law violations, including child-labor violations. A violation deemed to endanger a child's life or threaten moral values may be punished by temporary or permanent closure of the establishment. Nationwide labor inspectors are responsible for enforcing child labor laws. In 2014 the Ministry of Labor created the Child Labor Eradication Internal Working Group based in Bogota but with nationwide responsibilities to investigate cases of child labor and carry out activities to prevent child labor. It is unclear what actions this group has taken. Inspectors monitored the formal sector through periodic inspections, but an estimated 80 percent of all child labor occurred in the informal sector of the economy. Resources and training remained inadequate for effective enforcement.

Government agencies carried out several activities to eradicate and prevent exploitative child labor. With ILO assistance the government continued to improve cooperation among national, regional, and municipal governments through its national plan to eradicate child labor and protect working youth. It also continued to employ a monitoring system to register working children, although the system was not always regularly updated. The government also sought to reduce demand for child labor through public awareness and training efforts, often working with international and civil society organizations.

The government, through the Ministry of Labor, continued to follow the 2008 plan outlined in the National Strategy to Prevent and Eradicate the Worst Forms of Child Labor and Protect Young Workers. It also continued its roundtable discussion group, which includes government representatives, members of the three largest labor confederations, and civil society. The group concentrated its efforts on formalizing an integrated registration system for information on child labor that would permit public and private entities to register information about child workers. In August the government signed an agreement with the government of Cundinamarca Department and with the mayor of Pasto to prevent child labor and protect adolescent workers in the department and the city, respectively.

The government continued to combat illegal mining and formalize artisanal mining production, with the goal of eradicating child labor and forced labor. Regional ICBF offices were charged with leading efforts to combat child labor in mining at the local level, working with the Ministry of Labor and other government agencies to coordinate responses. The Department for Social Prosperity continued to implement the More Families in Action program to combat poverty through conditional cash transfers; it included a specific focus on addressing child labor. In interagency child labor meetings, the Ministry of Labor reported that whatever government presence was available in the area attended to children found working in illegal mining operations, whether police, the ICBF, teachers, or the DPS. While all agencies had directives on how to handle and report child labor cases, it was unclear whether all cases were referred to the ICBF.

The ICBF continued to implement several initiatives aimed at preventing child labor, including producing an extensive section of its website designed specifically for young audiences to educate children on child labor, their rights, and how to report child labor. The Ministry of Labor continued its work with the Network against Child Labor in which the ministry operates alongside member businesses that have pledged to work within the network to prevent and eradicate child labor.

Child labor remained a problem in the informal and illicit sectors. In April the National Administrative Department of Statistics (DANE) published the results of a 2015 survey of child labor that measured child labor during October-December 2014. DANE data noted that, of the 11.1 million children between ages five and 17, an estimated one million worked outside the home (approximately 68 percent boys and 32 percent girls). The national rate of children who worked outside the home was 9.1 percent, with 4.6 percent of children ages five to 14 working and 24.4 percent of children ages 15 to 17 working. For the period of the study, 32.8 percent of the children who worked did not attend school. According to the study, 48.3 percent of child laborers in urban areas engaged in commerce, hotel, and restaurant work, while 71.1 percent of child laborers in rural areas engaged in agriculture, fishing, cattle farming, hunting, and forestry work; 44.6 percent of working children ages five to 17 did not receive payment.

Significant incidences of child labor occurred in the production of clay bricks, coal, emeralds, gold, coca, and pornography. Children also worked as street vendors and domestic servants and were engaged in begging and garbage scavenging. There were also reports that children were involved in agriculture, including coffee production and small family production centers in the unrefined brown sugar market, as well as children selling inexpensive Venezuelan gasoline.

Commercial sexual exploitation of children occurred (see section 6, Children, Sexual Exploitation of Children).

Prohibitions against children working in mining and construction were reportedly largely ignored. Some educational institutions modify schedules during harvest seasons so that children may help on the family farm. Children worked in artisanal mining of coal, clay, emeralds, and gold under dangerous conditions and in many instances with the approval or insistence of their parents. The government's efforts to assist children working in illegal mining focused on the departments of Antioquia and Boyaca.

There continued to be instances of forced child labor in mines, quarries, and private homes. According to government officials and international organizations, illegal drug traders and other illicit actors recruited children, sometimes forcibly, to work in their illegal activities. The FARC, the ELN, and organized criminal gangs forced children into sexual servitude or to serve as combatants or coca pickers (see section 1.g.). Children working in the informal sector, including as street vendors, were also vulnerable to labor trafficking. The ICBF identified 819 children and adolescents who qualified for and received social services.

Also see the Department of Labor's *Findings on the Worst Forms of Child Labor* at www.dol.gov/ilab/reports/child-labor/findings/.

d. Discrimination with Respect to Employment and Occupation

The law prohibits discrimination in respect to employment or occupation regarding race, sex, religion, political opinion, national origin or citizenship, gender, disability, language, sexual orientation and/or gender identity, HIV-positive status or other communicable diseases, or social status. Complaints of quid pro quo sexual harassment are filed not with the Ministry of Labor but with the criminal courts. The government did not effectively enforce the law in all cases.

Unemployment disproportionately affected women. They faced hiring discrimination and received salaries that generally were not commensurate with their education and experience. According to DANE, only 55.8 percent of working age women were engaged in economic activity compared with 76.5 percent of men. Sisma Mujer reported on average women were paid 20.2 percent less than men. Among employees with a university education, women on average received between 11 and 23 percent less than the average wages of their male counterparts.

A senior government official estimated that 85 percent of persons with disabilities were unemployed.

e. Acceptable Conditions of Work

The minimum monthly wage as decreed by the government was COP 689,454 ($236) for all sectors. According to the national statistics authority, as of December 2015, 27.8 percent of the national population lived in poverty: 24.1 percent of the urban population and 40.3 percent of the rural population lived below the poverty line. The share of the national population living in extreme poverty was 7.9 percent.

The law provides for a regular workweek of 48 hours and a minimum rest period of eight hours within the week. Exceptions to this may be granted by the Ministry of Labor and were frequently found in the mining sector. The law provides for paid annual civil and religious holidays for all workers. Employees who work at least one full year are entitled to at least 15 days of paid vacation. The law stipulates that workers receive premium compensation for nighttime work, additional hours worked over the regular workweek of 48 hours, and work performed on Sundays. The law permits compulsory overtime only in exceptional cases where the work is considered essential for the company's functioning.

The law provides for workers' occupational safety and health in the formal sector. The legal standards were generally up to date and appropriate for the country's main formal industries. The law does not cover informal sector workers, including many mining and agricultural workers. In general the law protects workers' rights to remove themselves from situations that endanger health or safety without jeopardy to their employment, although some violations of this right were reported during the year. In cases of formal grievances, authorities generally protected employees in this situation.

The Ministry of Labor is required to enforce labor laws, including occupational safety and health regulations, in the formal sector through periodic inspections by labor inspectors. The government reported that as of August, the ministry employed 819 inspectors countrywide, although not all conducted worksite inspections and most have little training in occupational safety and health issues. Individual labor violations can bring fines of up to 5,000 times the minimum monthly wage, but infractions for occupational safety and health can receive fines of only up to 1,000 times the minimum monthly wage. Unionists stated that fines must be collected to achieve a formalized labor force. While the government's labor inspectors undertook administrative actions to enforce the minimum wage in the formal sector, the government remained unable to enforce the minimum wage in the informal sector.

To encourage the formalization of labor, the Ministry of Labor continued to promote formal employment generation. DANE defines an informal worker as one in any of the following seven situations, specifically excluding government workers: (1) workers in businesses that employ up to five individuals, including the owner/partner; (2) unremunerated family members working in establishments with five or fewer workers; (3) unpaid workers in businesses; (4) domestic workers in businesses with five or fewer workers; (5) day workers or task-specific workers in businesses with five or fewer workers; (6) self-employed workers in businesses with up to five persons, except independent professionals; and (7) employers in businesses of five or fewer workers. In the third quarter of the year, the proportion of informal workers was 47.8 percent. The government continued to support complementary social security programs to increase the employability of extremely poor individuals, displaced persons, and the elderly.

Nonunion workers, particularly those in the agricultural and port sectors, reportedly worked under hazardous conditions because they feared losing their jobs through subcontracting mechanisms or informal arrangements if they criticized abuses. Some unionized workers who alleged they suffered on-the-job injuries complained that companies illegally fired them despite existing legal protections designed to keep them from being fired. Only the courts may order reinstatement, and the workers complained the courts were backlogged, slow, and corrupt. The Ministry of Labor may sanction a company found to have broken the law in this way, but it may offer no other guarantees to workers.

Security forces reported that illegal armed actors, including the FARC, the ELN, and organized criminal groups, engaged in illegal mining of gold, coal, coltan, nickel, copper, and other minerals. Illegal mines were particularly common in the departments of Antioquia, Bolivar, Cauca, Cordoba, Choco, Narino, and Tolima.

According to the National Mining Agency, through July 31, there were 65 mine accidents reported, causing 59 miners' deaths. The majority of both accidents and deaths were due to cave-ins. There were no reports of non-mining major industrial accidents through October.